REMEMBERING DOCTOR LAWSON WILKINS:

A Pioneer of Pediatric Endocrinology

CLAUDE J MIGEON
ELIZABETH WILKINS MCMASTER

To our dear, longstanding friend, Pat Russell

Betsy

ISBN: 1497547601
ISBN 13: 9781497547605
Library of Congress Control Number: 2014906865
CreateSpace Independent Publishing Platform
North Charleston, South Carolina

PREAMBLE

Several tributes to Lawson Wilkins have been published. They include, but are not limited to:

- "To Honor Lawson Wilkins in His 65th Year." Edwards A. Park and Alfred M. Bongiovanni. The Journal of Pediatrics Vol.57, Number 3. 1957.

- "Presentation of the John Howland Medal and Award." Alfred M. Bongiovanni. The Journal of Pediatrics Vol.60, Number 4. 1960.

- "Acceptance of the Howland Award." Wilkins L.

- The Diagnosis and Treatment of Endocrine Disorders in Childhood and Adolescence. Charles C. Thomas Publishers. Springfield, Illinois.

    - Third Edition: John Money, PhD. 1965

    - Fourth Edition: Robert M. Blizzard, MD and Andrea Prader, MD 1994

- "Meeting Lawson Wilkins." Alfred Jost. The Johns Hopkins Medical Journal 130: 38. 1972.

- "Pediatric Profiles: Lawson Wilkins (1894-1963)." Robert M. Blizzard. The Journal of Pediatrics. Vol.133. pp. 577-580. October 1998.

- "The Early History of Pediatric Endocrinology." Delbert A. Fisher, MD and Zvi Laron, MD. Pediatric Endocrinology Reviews 1: 1. September 2003.

- Delbert A. Fisher. Pediatric Research 55. pp. 715. 2004.

However, the postdoctoral fellows of Lawson and some colleagues felt that something more substantial should be written by those who trained with him. In 2004, some of us met in Baltimore. A program of chapters to be covered by each of us was prepared. This effort was supported by Dr. Ann Johanson with the help of the Genentech Co. Unfortunately, it appears that none of us kept our promises and nothing constructive came out of it.

Dr. William Cleveland was anxious to make a report of the history of the Lawson Wilkins Pediatric Endocrine Society and of the beginning of the field throughout the United States. This also did not come to fruition due in part to the death of William.

The project was then taken up by Judson Van Wyk, but sadly it was cut short by Jud's death.

At this point in time, Betsy Wilkins McMaster and I decided that we should try again. We collected the papers of Jud Van Wyk and William Cleveland as well as old photographs that Barbara Migeon scanned into her computer.

Eventually, we decided that Betsy would write about the life of her father and mother. I would write about Dr. Wilkins and my life, as Lawson had been not only a mentor but also a father figure.

The present book is what came after two years of writing. My devotion, my admiration, my love for the man is very personal. However, I expect that the other fellows will identify with these feelings.

We also are writing for the next generation of pediatric endocrinologists so that they might know what a great mentor is and how to contribute to our field.

CHAPTER 1

LAWSON WILKINS: RECOLLECTIONS BY HIS DAUGHTER

Elizabeth Wilkins McMaster

CHAPTER 1

TABLE OF CONTENTS

1

INTRODUCTION

From my earliest childhood I always knew that my father, Lawson Wilkins, was a truly remarkable person. Unlike my friends' fathers who went to offices and did some vague kind of work, my father worked long and irregular hours at the most important work in the world—taking care of sick children, saving lives and doing detective work into mysterious illnesses. He relished hard work and mastering new subjects of all sorts, wanting to know all there was to know about the history or archeology of a place he was to visit, opera, whatever his children were studying. In his rare spare time, instead of playing golf, he liked to plunge into grueling work in his garden, ambitious cabinet work or ship model making. His favorite vacations before World War II were spent with friends, sailing the wilder regions of Chesapeake Bay, having exciting and fabulous adventures that became fodder for family legends and songs. He had a great range of friends and relished parties at home where, notoriously untalented in music, he would sing or play the violin with gusto or engage in hilarious, elaborately staged charades. He was a very loving father who made the brief vacations and days off memorable with raucous card games, patient lessons in fishing, sailing and swimming, and occasional excursions. Whatever he did or taught us, he demonstrated, rather than demanded, intellectual curiosity, thoroughness and one's very best effort. Add to these qualities a hearty—at times riotous—sense of humor and an irrepressible joie de vivre—and things were not dull when he was around. Most of all, he adored his "Lu," my mother who complemented all these qualities and truly made it possible for him to live his life as he did. And it was she who early explained to me that he was blessed to have as his core a calling that he so loved and that made it possible for him to live such a fulfilling life.

Lawson Wilkins was born on March 6, 1894, at 223 S. Broadway, Baltimore, Maryland. Presumably, his father, Dr. George Lawson Wilkins, an established physician, delivered him. His safe arrival must have been a cause of great rejoicing as the parents had previously lost two babies in infancy. Had they known what lay ahead for this baby, their joy and pride would have been immensely greater.

Lawson's father, known as "George" and "Lawson," had been born in or around Portsmouth, Virginia, in the tumultuous year of 1848. His family was said to have come from Ballyhack, a charming, small village near Waterford, on the southeast coast of Ireland. I do not know when or why they came to America. One family name was Lynch. One ancestor was reputedly named Pythagoras, perhaps a family legend. His father, Richard, was said to be an engineer; his mother's name is uncertain—thought to be Lydia. A charming daguerreotype shows George as a small boy with his sister, Mary Alice. His serious round face resembles that of his son, born almost forty years later. Family legend was that the family lived at Hampton Roads and George could have watched the battle of the Monitor and the Merrimac there in 1862. In truth, we know little about his family and childhood. Mary Alice married Norman Etheridge and I have names of her children and grandchildren with whom Lawson apparently had no contact or lost touch. We know nothing of how the family fared during or after the Civil War.

A sheepskin diploma in Latin declares that G. Lawson Wilkins received the degree of Doctor of Medicine at the University of Maryland in Baltimore, on March 10, 1870. Although founded in 1807, as part of a land grant university, this medical school was not in the forefront of medicine at the time. In the mid-nineteenth century, with the rapid expansion westward, the demand for doctors of all sorts had outpaced the supply. Many proprietary schools, with low or nonexistent standards, private businesses run by doctors, had sprung up. During the Civil War, both the city and the university were bitterly divided. This, combined with the competition, caused the medical school's enrolment to drop. When George Wilkins attended the school, the course in medicine lasted for two or three full years, unlike some of the "diploma mills" where the course was for six weeks only. It included anatomy learned using cadavers, unlike many other schools, and the student had to write and defend a dissertation.

After graduation, the new doctor did an apprenticeship of six to twelve months before setting up practice [1].

George Wilkins practiced general medicine in East Baltimore, which teemed with a variety of ethnic groups. Germans displaced by the revolutions of 1848 made up a large segment of the population, followed later by Poles, Lithuanians, Bohemians, Czechs, Italians and immigrants of many other countries, drawn to the second largest port in the United States, with its many industries. His office and home were presumably in the building at 223 South Broadway, which still stands, with an unusual wrought iron porch, reminiscent of Charleston.

In addition to his private practice, Dr. Wilkins was appointed the physician at the Baltimore City Jail, a position he held for many years. Newspaper clippings from the early 1880s contain colorful testimony he gave in proceedings to have a man accused of bigamy declared insane. An account of the death of a renowned robber in jail described the robber's last hours conversing with Dr. Wilkins who had become quite fond of him and remained with him until his death [2].

By 1882, Dr. Wilkins was a very active member of the Grand Lodge of the Ancient Order of United Workmen, a secret fraternal organization whose purpose was "to embrace and give equal protection to all classes and kinds of labor, mental and physical; to strive earnestly to improve the moral, intellectual and social conditions of its members... to create a fund for the benefit of its members during sickness or other disability, and in case of death to pay a stipulated sum to such person or persons... thus enabling him to guarantee his family against want."

On June 7, 1888, Dr. Wilkins married Harriet Isabel Schreiner in her mother's home in Philadelphia.

Figure 1. Dr. George Lawson Wilkins

3

We do not know how they met but we have many more facts about her early life than we have of his. Her family, of English, French and German descent, had been in Philadelphia since at least the early nineteenth century. Her mother, Mary Louise Fougeray, born in 1828, married Henry Schreiner in 1846. Mr. Schreiner had been married before and had at least four children. He had six more with his second wife and then apparently abandoned the family. There does not seem to have been much contact between Harriet and her older siblings in later life but she remained very close to her two younger sisters, Emilie and Clara.

Hattie, as she was always called, was born October 6, 1857. She graduated from the Girls' Normal School in Philadelphia and passed an examination qualifying to be a school principal. Life was apparently very hard for her mother and two young sisters. Hattie reportedly supported them by teaching. Emilie, five years younger, went to live in Philadelphia with an aunt and uncle, Jennie and Thomas Stokes, who were childless. Hattie was said to be quite musical and may have given piano lessons.

A photograph of the time of her marriage shows her to be a sweet-looking young woman with even features, wavy blond hair and a slight smile. She must have been tiny: when I was twelve years old and quite thin, I was allowed to dress up in her clothes—a white satin wedding dress and black velvet riding habit. Her shoes, two inches wide, and gloves were much too small for me and by the time I was thirteen I had outgrown the lovely dresses.

George and Hattie lived at 223 South Broadway. There is no indication from letters of any contact with either of their families or visits from them except for Hattie's two younger sisters and a few letters from cousins. There are many letters from Hattie's dear friend, Annie Baird Beaton, eleven years her junior, with whom she had been an active member of Bethany Presbyterian Church in Philadelphia. John Wanamaker, founder and owner of Wanamaker's department store, was superintendent of the Sunday school and took a lifelong interest in these two hardworking young women. George immediately became a dear friend of Annie's, too. When Hattie wrote to Annie, there was often a long postscript, signed "Doctor," "Lawson" or "Fadie" from him. These reveal a droll and affectionate sense of humor.

My grandfather always spoke adoringly of Hattie and they were apparently very happy together. Letters describe Hattie teaching a Sunday school class of boys, as she had in Philadelphia, chairing the Mission Board at Second Presbyterian Church and serving on the Board of Managers of the Presbyterian Home in 1889-90. She and the doctor belonged to a social club of professional people who met biweekly for socialization and education, such as lectures and music. Occasionally, friends and relatives came from Philadelphia for visits but there is only one mention of a visit from Hattie's mother and Hattie sometimes cautioned a correspondent not to let her mother know she had been to Philadelphia without visiting her and that her mother did not like some of her friends.

Their first child, Louise Person, named for a family friend, died in August of 1891, reportedly of dysentery. Their second baby, Russell Miller, named for a pastor of Hattie's church in Philadelphia, was born June 17, 1892. A letter to Annie, dated February 6, 1893, from George reports that Russell had broncho-pneumonia, that he feared it was "the forerunner of whooping cough" and not to tell Hattie's mother, so as not to worry her. A few days later the baby died and there are many letters of grief between the two friends.

At this time, when Baltimore and Philadelphia, among other cities, had open sewers and unsafe water supplies, when Pediatrics did not exist as a specialty and medicine had little to offer for childhood diseases, infant mortality was very high. For Hattie, now aged thirty-six and George, forty-five, the grief must have been profound. There are many letters from sympathetic relatives and friends, notably Hattie's friend and mentor, John Wanamaker, and the beloved minister, Russell Miller. Many expressed the view, voiced by Mr. Miller, that "a child in heaven is a more sacred tie than a child on earth" and that Hattie should think of Russell's death as "another of God's beautiful lessons. He is preparing you for a new and larger and sweeter service in the future. He has such training as this only when he is fitting his disciples for most delicate and honorable work. Your grief and sorrow have prepared your heart and hand for ministering to others in the days to come." Perhaps these were comforting words to Hattie, who obviously was a very devout woman, but that is not the view her son Lawson would have when he grew up; he could not believe a compassionate God inflicted such pain for such a purpose. In any case, Hattie had a very loving, sensitive and compassionate husband and they were soon to know greater happiness.

In 1893, my grandfather built an imposing four-story brick house almost on the crest of the hill at 6 North Broadway, just south of Johns Hopkins Hospital, with a stone foundation, corner turret with a balustrade on top, separate entrance to his medical office and a large garden behind it that made a statement of success and comfort. Photographs of the period show ornate dark woodwork, gaslit brass chandeliers, flocked wallpaper and formal Victorian furniture. At that time, Broadway was a fine place to live, (in spite of the sewers) with fountains in the grassy median and Patterson Park nearby. When I passed by in March of 2013, the house appeared to have been rehabilitated and was for sale. Since the 1940s, it had been a boarding house, a rooming house and then vacant for years

Figure 2. 6 North Broadway, home of Dr. George Lawson Wilkins

Figure 3. Harriet S. Wilkins
with baby Lawson

Figure 4. Lawson Wilkins age three

Lawson's birth on March 6, 1894, and healthy infancy must have seemed a God-sent joy to these loving parents. I know very little of his early childhood, except that he had happy memories of his parents. There were several servants and usually some hunting dogs as pets. In 1897, his sister, Emilie, was born. One of his early memories he humorously described as "having broken a leg in the Spanish-American War." As he was running down a long, highly polished hall, he collided with the incumbent pet, Lena, a Pointer—and fell

In 1900, Hattie was pregnant again. My grandfather later reported how thrilled Hattie was to have another baby but soon this happy family was plunged in grief. Six or seven months pregnant, Hattie was operated on for appendicitis. Shortly thereafter she was operated on again and the baby was taken. While apparently recovering, she developed septicemia and died. The renowned Drs. Halsted and Kelly had attended her. Lawson always grieved for the dear mother he had known. Emilie described a lifelong yearning for the mother she could not remember. No one has reported how my grandfather described his feelings at losing this patient, his wife, whom, like their first two babies, his medical skill could not save.

2

A CHILDHOOD OF SADNESS AND SUCCESS

During Hattie's confinements, losses of the babies and infancies of Lawson and Emilie, Hattie's sister, Clara, and their dear friend, Annie Beaton, spent time with her in Baltimore, although Clara worked for some years as a missionary teacher with Indians in Tucson, Arizona, and Annie had an office job with a land title company in Philadelphia.

Into this somber atmosphere, Aunt Clara Schreiner came to care for the bereaved children. Aside from her missionary work out west, there is no record of what work she had done. She had several mental breakdowns, apparently before and definitely after this period. According to my father, she subscribed to a very Calvinistic, "hellfire and brimstone" form of Presbyterianism. There was little joy in the home.

Two factors redeemed Lawson's childhood from absolute gloom. His father, whom those who knew him described as very similar to his son in adult life, was a wonderful companion to the little boy, teaching him carpentry and taking him hunting and fishing in nearby marshy and wooded outskirts of the city, now long since developed. Some days Lawson rode around with his father in his buggy as he made house calls and observed the doctor at work. He admired his father immensely and I do not know of a time when Lawson did not want to be a doctor, too. It is frustrating to know so little about my grandfather's life and education, as he was well-read and imparted much of this enthusiasm to his son. As my Aunt Emilie wrote in 1963 to Dr. Alfred Bongiovanni, one of Lawson's fellows, their father had "a vivid imagination and a great sense of humor, effervescent and kindly. He also liked colorful language. Characters from literature, especially Dickens and Thackeray, became alive in our household. When he felt the need of some strong expletive, which would be frowned upon by his wife, he would quickly couple his remarks with a so-called Shakespearean quotation. He also had some lesser but equally colorful expressions. He enjoyed driving the horse and buggy used professionally, or the 'trap' used for family rides, with squirming children in the rear. He drove with a flourish, whether on a cobblestoned street or up Broadway, with its flowering park, overhanging trees, and fountains, to the country just beyond North Avenue. However, Dad not only felt he should have absolute right-of-way but loudly called the wrath of Shakespeare with a few additions of his own upon anyone who chose to be upon the street"[3]. Lawson reported that his father addressed the offenders as "wild and woolly elephants" or "thou false Rodrigo villain, thou!"

The example of a father who had educated himself without apparent support from his family and made a prominent place for himself in the community was not lost on his son. The questioning mind that led to research was there. Also, Dr. Wilkins published a paper on the need to use a thermometer to measure a fever accurately, as opposed to feeling the patient's brow and estimating the temperature as was then the custom.

On October 1, 1870, when my grandfather was barely out of medical school, the following article appeared in *The Baltimore Sun* [4]:

> Cancer from Smoking—In the early part of this week Dr. G. Lawson Wilkins, assisted by Charles McCormick, a medical student, operated for the removal of a cancer of the lower lip on Mr. James Ewings of Canton Avenue. Mr. Ewings, who is an inveterate smoker, first noticed the appearance of the disease on the right side of the lower lip (the side he usually smokes on) over a year ago.

The other factor that enlivened Lawson's life and contributed to his success was his education. Not satisfied with the public schools he saw in East Baltimore, my grandfather persuaded some of his neighbors to join him in hiring a carriage to take their children across town to the Baltimore Friends School that had recently moved into fine stone buildings in the 1700 block of Park Avenue with some of the best facilities in Baltimore—state-of-the-art science laboratories, art rooms, library, gym, showers and, very soon, a swimming pool.

Lawson and Emilie both went to Friends School from kindergarten through twelfth grade, Lawson skipping two grades in early elementary school although he still said "grandmuvver" for "grandmother." Both felt it was the best schooling they could have had and the gentle, principled atmosphere of Quaker education was a solace to these motherless children. While my father never subscribed to the Quaker philosophy, my experience with Quaker education leads me to believe that it had a lifelong influence on him. Baltimore had had a substantial Quaker community since 1656 and, to provide a "guarded education" for their children, a Friends school had been founded in 1784—the first school in the city, forty-five years before the first public school. The Quakers stressed equality of all people, believing "there is that of God in every man," as well as simplicity in all things and nonviolence. They emphasized perfectionism in all aspects of life and as a goal for society. The school had always accepted outsiders as well as Quakers and the students were generally children of professional people and prosperous merchants, college bound, but not the social elite of the city [4]. Lawson's elementary education included French, German, painting, drawing, calisthenics, instrumental music and voice culture! Heaven only knows how that contributed to his later singing ability.

3

THE BALTIMORE FIRE

At 10:48 a.m. on Sunday, February 7, 1904, the Baltimore Fire Department received an automatic alarm of a fire at a business in the heart of downtown Baltimore. By noon Baltimore was experiencing a devastating fire that lasted thirty hours and destroyed seventy square blocks. 1500 buildings, including many of the major banks and businesses, were reduced to ashes.

At home the neighborhood was showered with sparks and for hours my father's family expected to be forced from their house. All night, a terrified Aunt Clara kept Lawson, aged nine, and Emilie, six, at the third floor window, praying. Finally the wind shifted and they could see that their prayers were answered: the house was out of danger.

Meanwhile, my grandfather was having an even more exciting time. I have a letter, dated two days later from him to "Sister Mary," (who was most likely Hattie's half sister with whom they had some communication) with a vivid description of the fire.

"Six North Broadway

February 9, 1904

Dear Sister Mary,

Your letter came this morning. Many thanks for your kind interest and sympathy. I am worn out but will attempt to write. Thank God we escaped. For some hours great sparks flooded this section, but fortunately the wind shifted and we were out of immediate danger. We were up all Sunday night and did not know at what hour we might be compelled to leave our home. The Phil. papers are giving full descriptions so I will not write anything in detail. The calamity is simply beyond human conception. You must come to Balto. and see the devastation and ruins of our city. The very heart and the very pride of Balto. is destroyed. The paper sent is but a small copy printed in Washington but you will find a facts map of the burnt district. Every newspaper in Balto. every Trust Bldg. and many leading banks are gone. 150 or 200 blocks of the very richest part of Balto. are destroyed. The people of the city are very grateful for the help sent from Phil. and our sister cities.

The fire started about 11 a.m. and on receiving reports of the terrible destruction going on, I went to the scene of the disaster. I got there about 3 p.m. and remained until after midnight. The police admitted me within all the lines and I witnessed the destruction of many of the leading buildings. I got in with a number of the Reporters and went with them from one point to another. At the start the wind was from the S.W. and the track of the fire was at first N.E. When the fire reached the cor. Charles and Lexington the wind shifted and blew a gale from the N.W. This led the fire to take a S.E. course and the fire consumed all the great Trust Bank and newspaper bldgs. Whilst the shifting of the wind drove the hurricane of fire in the direction of so many great buildings, at the same time it drove it to the water front and made it possible for the firemen to arrest it. The first direction would have given the fire 6 or 7 miles of houses to feed upon instead of about 1 ½ miles. The first course would have involved more suffering of the people, if not such a great money loss. I wish that I could convey to you some of the thrilling experiences on the first night of the fire, but time forbids, so I shall limit myself to the bare relation of just one of the many thrilling sights. About midnight, I was standing on the N.W. corner of Fayette and North Sts. In company with Gov. Warfield and Mr. Furst. The wind was then blowing a gale. Directly west of us stood the Equitable and Calvert Bldgs., a little to the S.W. the B. and O., Carrolton Hotel together with many surrounding bldgs were all at one time going down in the terrible tornado of fire. As we watched this awe-inspiring sight, a great stream of fire and burning brands extending from curb to curb and a foot deep, came sweeping down Balto. St. like a great snow drift or a great river of water. At the corner of Balto. St, this stream of fire seemed to divide into two great streams, one going down South St. and the other going east on Balto. St. but both coursing on in their errand of ruin and destruction, with fury and without mercy.

God grant that such a fire may never again happen in this world's history! What the ultimate effect will be no one can say at this time.
We all send love,

Your affectionate Brother
George L Wilkins"

His impulsive desire to be in the center of a historic event sounds like the sort of response Lawson might have made under similar circumstances. Upon receiving word of the conflagration downtown, he ran about a mile and a quarter to the scene and, joining a group of reporters, followed the fire at very close range as the winds swept it through the heart of the business district. As physician at the city jail since 1900, he was well known to the police. He was granted access to the front line and at times stood watching with the governor and other dignitaries.

4

THE STEPMOTHER

In 1905, the Wilkins household noticed that Dr. Wilkins made many mysterious telephone calls to Philadelphia—an unusual thing for that era. In April, Dr. Wilkins's friends and patients were surprised to learn that he had married his dear friend, Annie B. Beaton, of Philadelphia and set out for Europe on a wedding trip. Aunt Clara probably suspected the romance—she had filled Lawson and Emilie's ears with stories of wicked stepmothers. Perhaps she hoped to marry her sister's widower instead.

A shy woman of thirty-eight with little experience with children other than the Sunday school classes she had taught, Annie seemed ill-equipped to be a stepmother. My father and Aunt Emilie said they never felt any warmth from her. The daughter of Scots, she was a strict Presbyterian with staid ways. In defiance, Lawson and Emilie would run home from church on Sunday mornings to play one record on the gramophone before Annie got there. My grandfather took to keeping his bottle of whisky in his galoshes in the hall closet and tried to control his explosive outbursts and humor. She and my grandfather had a marriage of thirty years and my father and aunt were dutiful children but I always felt a tension between her and us.

My father seemed to excel at all he did in school. He learned French, German and Latin and pulled out his notebooks of impeccable translations of Caesar, Cicero and Virgil when I was studying the same material more than forty years later, not to provide help (it must be all my own work) but to enjoy recalling his classical education. He loved the sciences and retained long passages of the literature he had read all his life. Although slight of build, about 110-115 pounds, he played on the basketball and lacrosse teams. He held various class offices and edited the school newspaper and yearbook. He was popular and made many lifelong friends, including Felix Morley, an author and editor, later president of Haverford College, and a number of children of the successful German Jewish merchants who were making important places for themselves in Baltimore [5].

Emilie felt she had a sadder childhood than Lawson and resented his greater freedom. She, too, appreciated what Friends School offered and made lifelong friends there but was more tied to home. She felt her father wanted her to sit at his knee and let him stroke her golden curls, like a perfect Victorian daughter. She had to fight to go to college, move away from home and create a career.

My grandfather did not neglect Lawson and Emilie's musical education, either. One of his patients was Austin Conradi, the first violinist in the Baltimore Symphony Orchestra. In lieu of paying his medical bills, my grandfather asked Mr. Conradi to teach Lawson the violin and Emilie the piano. After a year or so, Mr. Conradi beseeched my grandfather to let him go back to paying his bills and to be relieved of teaching Lawson and Emilie. Despite this diagnosed lack of musical ability, my father, in his perfectionist way, had mastered the fingering and bowing of the violin. Thirty or so years later, when I undertook to learn the viola, my father picked it up and was able to play to the extent that my mother bought him a secondhand violin and, with her good piano playing holding us together, we happily made some excruciating music together.

Lawson and Emilie's singing was notorious, also, but whereas Emilie avoided occasions when she might have to sing, Lawson loved to join in or lead with his extraordinarily deep bass whenever a singing party could be stirred up. In adult life he enjoyed the symphony and opera, too.

5

HIGH SCHOOL AND COLLEGE

I have much less information about Lawson's high school and college years than about his early life. He completed high school in three years by taking extra courses each year. There was apparently no question of his going away to college and he was proud and happy to have gone to Johns Hopkins University. He made many friends, joined Phi Gamma Delta fraternity, may have played lacrosse and continued to excel at academic endeavors. In my childhood, he would tell funny stories about lab experiments and would hold forth, reciting Chaucer, Shakespeare and Milton at length at the dinner table. One summer he taught daily vacation Bible school (perhaps under pressure from his stepmother) and another year he waited tables at a resort in the Poconos. Such experiences were interspersed with tales of dances, picnics, canoe trips and mountain climbing. He graduated from college in 1914, Phi Beta Kappa.

The medical school curriculum Lawson studied was much longer, more rigorous and scientific than his father had. Johns Hopkins University had been founded in 1873, opened in 1876. With its emphasis on graduate schools and de-emphasis of the distinctions between graduate and undergraduate work, many considered it the first truly American university. Following a half century of efforts by the American Medical Association Committee on Medical Education and the Association of America Medical Colleges to raise the standards among medical schools, the founding of Johns Hopkins Medical School in 1893 marked the start of a new sort of medical education with higher standards. A four-year college degree was required for entry; there was a four year curriculum; the school year lasted a full nine months; there were teaching laboratories and integrated college and hospital facilities to provide clinical training for advanced medical students. The Flexner Report of 1910, "Medical

Education in the United States," showed up the inadequacies of most medical schools, many of which closed while others improved their curricula; Johns Hopkins was the model.

Starting medical school in 1914, Lawson was in the best place at a very exciting time. William Osler had left Hopkins in 1905; I do not know which of the three other "greats," William H. Welch, William S. Halsted or Howard A. Kelly, my father had contact with but he knew medical history was being made [6].

6

WORLD WAR I

A lthough the United States was still neutral early in 1917, there was a strong sentiment for sending an American Expeditionary Force to assist the Allies. Almost at the last moment, it was decided to include personnel for one base hospital. At first, under the direction of the Red Cross, such medical units later came under control of the Army Medical Corps. Starting in May, Dr. Winford Smith, director of the Hopkins Hospital, rapidly developed plans to send staff, volunteers and material to create such a hospital. Within the month this had been put into effect. The concerns of the medical school faculty as to whether to accept third year medical students as volunteers were resolved by plans to provide the students with academic work overseas and to award their diplomas at the end of a year.

After a five day wait in New York, this hastily assembled crew of doctors, nurses, thirty-two medical students, cooks, stenographers, plumbers, carpenters, and so forth, led by Dr. J.M.T. Finney, set sail as part of a convoy on June 14, 1917 Following a circuitous route to avoid submarines, they arrived in the port of St. Nazaire, France, on June 18. After a few days in the nearby town of Savenay, the unit traveled by train to Bazoilles, a small town in the Vosges Mountains in the

Figure 5. Lawson Wilkins in Johns Hopkins Medical Unit, 1917

east of France, arriving July 26. Taking over a one thousand-bed temporary hospital, the members of the unit quickly prepared it for use. About eighty miles southeast of Reims, the hospital was near the battlegrounds of the Marne and Verdun. My father never told us about the wounded he saw but had colorful tales of the poilus, Senegalese and other colonials he saw. He spoke of his distress at the death of two medical students and several nurses, who died of communicable diseases and their complications.

The students functioned as junior interns, anesthetists, assistants and laboratory technicians. They attended lecture courses by Johns Hopkins staff members and a course in Langres on the organization and administration of the Medical Corps, special problems of troop sanitation, the evacuation of the wounded and other responsibilities of the medical officers.

In April of 1918, Dr. Finney received a cable from the dean of the medical school announcing the graduation of all the medical students. As Lawson told it, the bugle blew for them to line up, Dr. Finney read the telegram granting them their degrees and then commanded them back to whatever they had been doing—Lawson had been cleaning bedpans. Later they were commissioned as first lieutenants.

Following the November 11, 1918 armistice, the Base 18 unit left Bazoilles on January 20, 1919. They sailed from St. Nazaire on February 1 and were discharged in New Jersey on February 20 [7].

While Lawson told his family little of the horrors of war, his nineteen months left him a lifelong Francophile. In his photograph album, in addition to snapshots of his comrades, the ships and hospital, there are many pictures of French villages, chateaux, soldiers, workmen and well-dressed civilians who sometimes entertained the visiting Americans. He especially loved the coast of Brittany and was thrilled to show me the places he had visited during his stay in St. Nazaire more than thirty years earlier.

7

EARLY CAREER

When Lawson returned from France, it was too late to obtain an internship at Johns Hopkins. He took an internship in internal medicine at Yale-New Haven Hospital—the only time in his career when he worked away from Baltimore.

The following year he accepted an internship in pediatrics at Hopkins. Still looking slim and boyish, by 1926 he grew a moustache to enhance his maturity and credibility. I know little about his early days of practice and work in the clinics at the Harriet Lane Home, the pediatric wing of the Johns Hopkins Hospital.

I do have evidence of his social life and good times in his photograph album. Like many of his fellow soldiers he stayed in the reserve or National Guard, attending camp at Tobyhanna, Pennsylvania, in the summers and spent time riding horseback. By 1925 he had acquired a sailboat, a twenty-five-foot catboat with a twelve-foot beam, into whose cockpit he crammed crowds of friends. How much he knew about sailing before that, I do not know, but there were later tales of crazy cruises, groundings and surviving wild storms on Chesapeake Bay. Sailboats were a part of his life from then on.

In this era of Prohibition and despite his stepmother's upbringing, liquor was always available for the good times, reportedly some bathtub gin. He combined his chemical expertise and his French experience to try to manufacture Grand Marnier, with some success—he claimed.

In addition to his old friends from school and medical school, he made many new friends, some parents of his pediatric patients, some in academia at Hopkins, on the staff of *The Baltimore Sun* and in various businesses. Some were from Goucher College, friends of his younger sister, Emilie—and that may have been how he met Lucile Mahool.

8

MARRIAGE

I do not know how or when my mother and father met. Her photograph album contains a number of pictures of Lucile riding horseback in Howard County with a long-term beau and with a group of friends at Cape May, both in 1925. Lucile and Lawson were married June 9, 1926—(perhaps after a whirlwind romance?)

My father said that, because of his puritanical upbringing, he had determined to marry "the most worldly woman" he could find—if not a Catholic, an Episcopalian. They were married in what they described as the cellar of the Episcopal Cathedral of the Incarnation, (the undercroft), as construction of the cathedral was just beginning. There was a reception at the Mahools' house in Roland Park, where there was some dissimulation about the punch, as the Mahools were teetotalers also, although not with the ferocity of Mrs. Wilkins's beliefs. Perhaps Lawson's father helped out.

My mother and father always seemed to adore each other and complemented each other remarkably. My mother, six years my father's junior, came from families who had been in Baltimore and Baltimore County at least since the eighteenth century. Aside from an uncle who could not get elected to a second term as mayor of Baltimore because he was "too honest," no one had done anything extraordinary. My maternal grandparents and their three children lived on 29th Street with Aunt Bessie and Uncle Horatio, my grandmother's siblings, until 1923 when, with Uncle Horatio's help, they bought a lovely house at the top of Merrymount Road in Roland Park. Her family life seemed happy and secure, with numerous relatives around, trips to the mountains and beach, ice skating in the winter and tennis in the park. She had a brother four years younger and a sister eight years younger.

Lucile, called "Lu" by all her family and friends, had pretty, regular features, a radiant smile and fine brown hair that turned gray very young. Her ladylike demeanor masked a merry, at times wicked, sense of humor; everyone found her to be loads of fun and she was very popular. As my grandmother enjoyed bragging, "You know, she had eleven proposals—eleven DEFINITE proposals!"

Lucile graduated from Western High School, the academically oriented girls' high school of the day, and Goucher College with a BA in French and Spanish. She played the piano quite well and loved gathering people around to sing. She was the first member of her family to go to college and the first to go abroad, taking a chaperoned tour of Europe in 1923. She taught kindergarten and first grade and was teaching at Baltimore Friends School when she got married.

The newlyweds had a honeymoon in Bermuda where Lawson distinguished himself by falling in the water in his white flannel trousers; when the rigging on their rented sailboat fouled, he immediately climbed the mast to fix it, not realizing this boat did not have the stability of his beamy old *Typhoon*, leaving Lucile shrieking and visualizing herself a widow.

They settled in the Calvert Court Apartments on Calvert Street where Lucile said she had a great deal to learn about cooking. In those days, and until World War II, she phoned Mr. Lissey at the Wyman Park Market every morning, as did her mother, to ask him what looked good and to have him send her order over. They had a cook until World War II and a laundress two days a week.

9

CHILDREN

On September 23, 1927, George Lawson Wilkins, II, was born. He was always called "Skippy;" my father was the captain of the ship and his son was to be the skipper. He was a merry, high-spirited little boy.

The stock market crash of 1929 and the Depression caused belt-tightening and anxiety for my parents. Even if my father was pretty well established as a practicing pediatrician, not all of his patients' families were. When the banks closed, some people came to pay their bills in cash, thinking first of the doctor to whom they were grateful. Others provided produce from their farms or firewood. Few did not try to pay, except the Gypsy King, who skipped town after his daughter recovered from her pneumonia, for which my father had made daily visits.

My father sold his boat and gave up memberships in the Baltimore Country Club and the Gibson Island Club. He never joined again after the Depression; country clubs did not appeal to him. He and my mother were frugal and I always felt they had anxiety left from the Depression years.

I was born October 11, 1931, and named Elizabeth Biays after an ancestor of my mother's. My family was living in an apartment in Roland Park in the home of Dr. and Mrs. Frank Ford who had become dear friends. We soon moved to a rented house a few blocks away where we lived until 1939 when my father bought the house on Edgevale Road where he lived until his death.

Roland Park, one of the first planned communities in the country, was designed by the firm of Frederick Olmstead in the 1890s. The streets and footpaths followed the hilly contours of the land. There was a variety of housing, mostly shingle style or English cottage style, including imposing mansions, large comfortable houses, more modest homes, double houses and an apartment house, all designed by architects. Some enclosed lots were left empty for playgrounds and there were some large wooded areas. Many streets were lined with elms. I took all this for granted as a child but, as an adult, came to realize what an idyllic neighborhood it was for children.

10

LAWSON RELAXING

I have many distinct memories of my early childhood but saw little of my father; reading of his involvement with specialty clinics in addition to his burgeoning practice, I understand why he usually came home after my bedtime, had to see patients on Saturdays and Sundays and slept late on Sundays. Spare time on weekends he usually spent working strenuously in his garden, no matter how hot the day. Some nights, when not studying, he worked into the wee hours on elaborate ship models. He often complained of severe headaches (migraine or stress?) which he treated with pyramidon, a very powerful painkiller that is no longer available in this country. If home in the early evening, he usually took a brief nap on our hard Empire sofa and was then reinvigorated for serious work until one or two in the morning, a habit my aunt has described from his school days.

Into this busy schedule, he managed to fit time to attend the visiting Philadelphia Orchestra and Metropolitan Opera with my mother, often arriving home in the nick of time to don his tuxedo and gobble a sandwich in the car. And then there were the parties, often impromptu, with singing around the loaned piano (with a cracked soundboard) tactfully accompanied by my musical mother and lubricated by plenty of drink. Favorites were from Gilbert and Sullivan, Negro spirituals, The Scottish Student's Songbook, The Book of a Thousand Songs and, especially, rowdy sea chantries, all sung lustily with Lawson's basso profundo, sometimes on-tune! Friends of all sorts were mixed in these gatherings and shy or unfamiliar foreign visitors were invariably swept into the musicale. (Never in my or my mother's presence did he perform any of the reportedly ribald standards sung at the medical students' Pithotomy Club.)

Other memorable evenings in my early childhood were devoted to our version of charades, not the silent miming of later years but elaborate, spontaneous, costumed performances of complicated or abstruse words. In the attic was a large box of costumes not only for the children to dress up in but for the adult games. I have a very early memory of the young Dr. George Thorn, (who later became the Professor of Medicine at Harvard Medical School,) waking me to locate my father's army uniform for a charade in which he was a telegraph boy delivering bad news—rather frightening for a small, sleepy child who could not quite yet distinguish drama from reality. A cheerier charade involved a lady draped on our Empire sofa as Cleopatra while my father portrayed Caesar with a garbage can lid for a shield. As with the singing parties, sleep upstairs was impossible, anyway, so we children came down in our pajamas and were often incorporated into the drama.

My father really knew how to let down his hair and have a rip-roaring good time and his enthusiasm was impossible to resist.

Perhaps Lawson's most relaxed and joyous times in prewar days were cruising vacations on the Chesapeake Bay. After giving up the *Typhoon* in 1931, my parents and friends chartered larger sailboats for cruises. Beginning in 1934 they cruised each summer on the *Richard J. Vetra*, a fifty-two-foot Chesapeake Bay oyster workboat that had been converted into a sailing pleasure boat (I couldn't describe it as a yacht) by his boon companion, Milton Offutt. Milt, a former *Baltimore Sun* reporter, was now a professor of history of science at City College of New York. He and his wife had a summer place on the Severn River. Milt was a brilliant, bitter, eccentric, opinionated and very funny man who had a great influence on my childhood. My parents spent two weeks each summer with him and his wife on the then seventy-year-old *Vetra*, exploring remote areas of the Chesapeake and its tributaries, which were quite isolated in those days. Milt and my father would stay up very late, drinking, discussing science and philosophy and solving the problems of the world. Milt sang almost as well as my father and each summer my parents returned with new songs (in the fifties I discovered we were all folk singers!) including some Milt had written over the winter to describe escapades of the previous summer and highly embellished accounts of their adventures.

After the adults-only cruise (which included Milt's daughter, eight years my senior), when we had been left in the care of our grandparents or another willing relative, the family would spend two weeks in a rented cottage on the Severn River. The thirty-mile trip from Baltimore was a wild journey. My father usually was visiting patients till the last minute when the four Wilkinses would pile into the cars (my mother had a 1929 Model A Ford with a rumble seat), with the cook, boxes of food for the vacation, the Irish setter and whatever assorted cats were currently family members. The latter usually escaped from the hat box in which they were traveling, along with assorted bugs and bees that flew in the open windshield, wreaking havoc among the passengers.

The summer cottages varied wildly. Before leaving home, my father gave us typhoid fever shots. In my earliest memories there was a cramped cottage with a pump for iron-flavored water, a frightening outhouse and neighbors who constantly played one record, "Flat Foot Floogie (with a Floy Floy)." Another summer we were in a naval officer's mansion outside Annapolis. It ran the gamut but we always had fun. We swam and floated for hours in inner tubes in the warm, brackish water. We crabbed and fished for perch, sunfish and the occasional striped bass off the dock. We dug clay from the beach and sculpted. We walked to nearby farms for corn and tomatoes and made sightseeing and shopping excursions to Annapolis.

My father had an eleven-foot dinghy, sister ship to Milt's, built for us and taught us to sail. As the smallest, my position in the crew was to sit in the bottom, shift my slight weight and dodge the boom. I came to love sailing much later. No matter how primitive the quarters, my parents always invited Baltimore friends to come for a picnic and cooling swim, often staying on for singing parties on the dock where the harmony sounded even better.

Dad devoted himself with his usual intensity to these activities with us. Among the most memorable were the wild rainy-day games of Demon Pounce, a loose form of multiple solitaire where everyone was playing all the time and playing on other people's cards, too, with lots of pushing and shouting. In a quieter vein, my parents and grandparents taught us to play bridge.

Christmas Eve, Dad usually did not get home till the stockings had been hung and we were in bed. He would bring from the basement an eight-by-eight-foot wooden platform he had built, cover it with fresh moss and set the Christmas tree on it. The tree was decorated with old ornaments from his childhood and some new ones. Then he and my mother went to work creating the Christmas garden. My grandmother's doll house stood in one corner, a German manger scene in another. Through the garden ran the track of Skippy's Lionel train, a mirror formed a pond and every year the collection of little English lead figures—farm animals, villagers, workmen—increased. When we descended on Christmas to see the lighted tree with the train circling it, we were enchanted. One Christmas "Santa" had a broken rib from falling off a ladder putting the angel on top of the tree. One year he had embellished the lovely eight-room dollhouse that Grandfather Wilkins had built for me when I was three; Dad put in electric lights and nice woodwork, including stairs with tiny handrails and newel posts. My mother had wallpapered and made little curtains and rugs.

Christmas gardens were a Baltimore tradition because of the large German population. In addition to visiting those of friends, my father took us to the fire stations around town where the firemen had created large and wonderful gardens for visitors to enjoy.

Another family outing was to the circus. When I was about five, we were taken to meet Jack Earl, the "Texas Giant." Dad had gone to the circus grounds early in the morning to ask Jack Earl for a urine specimen for his developing endocrine research. When he returned for the performance with Mother and us children, he was sorely disappointed that the specimen barely covered the bottom of the gallon jug he had optimistically left. He expected much more from a giant! On that trip he introduced me to many of the midgets and dwarves in the side show; looking into those wizened, prematurely aged faces was a shock to a five-year-old. The first introduction to my father's interesting specialty made for good stories at kindergarten. (I did not tell my friends about the kittens whose thyroids he had experimentally removed so that they always looked like babies.)

11

FAMILY

It is obvious what a devoted father Lawson was but because he could not spend very much time with us, as a child I was much closer to my mother. She was wonderful at storytelling, singing, helping with dress-ups, puppets and plays, giving children's parties with different themes and taking me to museums, concerts, plays and so forth The other big influence in our house

Figure 6. Wilkins family, 1935

Figure 7. Lawson Wilkins, 1938

was Mary Johnson, the black cook, who worked for us from the time I was two until she left to work in a parachute factory during World War II. Having no children, she welcomed me into the kitchen where she taught me nursery rhymes, Negro spirituals, and lots of cooking. When my mother was out doing volunteer work for the YWCA, Community Chest, Johns Hopkins Hospital and other charities or playing bridge or attending the garden club, Mary and I had a glorious time in the kitchen.

Skippy, being four years older, seemed from another generation. He was very active with many friends playing cops and robbers, cowboys and Indians, football and pranks where a little sister was a nuisance. I was much shyer, playing dolls, dressing up and such with one or two other little girls at a time.

Like his father before him, Lawson sent his children to the best private schools he could find, although the local public school was quite good. Skippy went to Roland Park Country School (RPCS) through fourth grade as it took boys as well as girls to accommodate families in those pre-two-car-family days. Then, with many classmates, he went on to the Gilman Country School. He did not thrive in its rigidly academic atmosphere and about seventh grade my parents transferred him to Baltimore Friends School, which was more relaxed and understanding. He loved it. In adult life, I have wondered if Skip had a mild learning disability as he frequently had to be tutored; on the other hand, with his extroverted personality and many boyish interests, he may have just not seen the point in being too interested in his studies.

I went to RPCS from kindergarten through twelfth grade where, as a depression baby, I benefitted from very small classes; tuitions were extremely low as the private schools were struggling to stay open through the hard times and even gave discounts to families of doctors, teachers and clergy who were considered to be struggling on small salaries.

The Mahool grandparents lived nearby and we saw a great deal of them. My mother phoned her mother every day and my father remained devoted to his in-laws for life.

My Grandfather Wilkins had built a large house in the new development of Guilford in the 1920s. The sun porch there was his office where he saw patients until about a week before his death at the age of eighty-six. Dad took on some of his father's very elderly patients and sometimes took me on his home visits to them; they doted on him and enjoyed seeing the beloved doctor's four-year-old granddaughter.

My Grandmother Wilkins stayed on in the house on 39th Street, cared for by a faithful housekeeper till her death in 1945. My father managed her affairs and was always a responsible son. We saw a good deal of her.

My father's sister married and lived in Pennsylvania; her family would visit Baltimore about once a year. My mother's only sister married and lived in Pennsylvania also and visited frequently with her two sons who were considerably younger than me. Uncle Tom, my mother's bachelor brother, lived a few blocks away with my grandparents.

12

WORLD WAR II

Our parents kept us aware of current events and in elementary school I knew that bad things were happening in Europe. When I was quite small I recall my parents allowed me to hear a speech by Hitler on the shortwave radio, explaining what an evil man he was.

In 1938 Dr. Walter Fleischmann, a Viennese physiologist, came to work in my father's laboratory. Although I remember him and his family well, I never knew much about him or how he came to Baltimore. This spring (2013) after a hiatus of more than fifty years, I have been in touch with his daughter, Ruth Fleischmann Weiner, who has kindly provided me with information about Dr. Fleischmann and his family, from what her father told her.

"Walter was in Chicago at some sort of international medical meeting in the spring of 1938 and was advised by colleagues there to get his family out as soon as possible. I believe Lawson Wilkins offered Walter an appointment at Hopkins at that time. At any rate, he stayed in the US and got visas for my mother and me and we sailed on the Westernland from Antwerp to New York in October of 1938—a month before my fourth birthday—and went by train to Baltimore. (I still have my green card, by the way.) In effect, Lawson Wilkins saved the lives of the Fleischmann family.

"Walter had quite a respectable publications list from his research in Vienna—a Festschrift was done for him in 1970 and I have many of the German language publications. "Walter's parents and siblings" (a brother and two sisters) "and their families emigrated at that time to England." (Ruth informed me that Walter's father, a physician in Vienna, had been a good friend of Sigmund Freud and had delivered his daughter, Anna.) "My mother, Gertrude, tried to bring her parents out but thanks to the US State Department she could not get visas for them. In 1942 they were deported to Riga, shot by the Nazis, and lie in a mass grave somewhere in Latvia. Neither Walter nor Gertrude ever knew what happened to them; I only learned a couple of years ago in a letter from the Austrian archives.

"My half-brother, Wolfgang Bernard, (who went by Bernard in the US) was living with his mother in France and was brought out by the American Unitarian Fellowship in 1940, along with fifteen other Jewish children who had relatives in the US. Walter got Bernie's mother out, as well as some more distant cousins. Bernie lived with us; his mother lived in New York and eventually went back to Vienna. Bernie died very suddenly in 1987 of heart disease; his mother actually outlived him by a year or so. My mother died in 1947 of breast cancer that had been in remission.

"I started school at Baltimore Friends School because I knew no English at all...I was fluent in both languages in a couple of months. We had very little money and I went to public school after third grade. Sometime after the war Walter got a position at Army Chemical Center at Edgewood though he kept up his connection with the Harriet Lane Home. (Claude Migeon would have a better sense of the timeline than I.) Actually Walter put me to work in the Harriet Lane when I was still in high school, doing flame photometry. Eventually Walter became certified in pathology and was pathologist at several VA hospitals in Baltimore, North Carolina and Tennessee. He married Sisanne Kann (yet another PhD) who continued to work with him. He worked and published until his diabetic retinopathy and atherosclerosis got bad enough that he could no longer work. He died in Johnson City, Tennessee, in 1979. Susanne Kann Fleischmann died in 1997."

Ruth Fleischmann Weiner has a PhD in chemistry and has had a very successful career. She lives in Albuquerque and works at Sandia National Laboratory. She has four daughters, is in touch with her relatives in England and has enjoyed revisiting Vienna [8].

Another Austrian refugee my parents helped to settle here was Dr. Walter Block, whose wife, Elsa, was a gentile, a cousin of the opera star, Lotte Lehmann. They had a small son, Peter. Again my parents provided hospitality until they were settled in. Dr. Block developed a medical practice, also, and stayed in Baltimore.

In September 1939, our parents took us to the World's Fair in New York. The B & O train ride, the hotel, the subway to Flushing and everything about the fair was thrilling to me but I was aware of a pervading sadness as my parents pointed out the closed pavilions of Czechoslovakia and Poland, and the worried atmosphere in the French, Dutch and Belgian displays.

When the war came, Lawson, in his late forties, was too old to enlist but I saw less of him than ever. He covered the practices of several other younger pediatricians, who were away in the service. He rose at seven when the phone would start ringing incessantly. Receiving forty or more calls during breakfast, he grew to hate the telephone and let forth a stream of oaths before answering each time. My mother was in terror that he would not stop swearing before picking up the phone but he always sounded calm and collected when he did. During my years with him, I heard a great deal of creative blasphemy and rage, but never sexual or scatological language. In between calls, he would mournfully address his breakfast: "Oh, little fried egg, shall I never be allowed to eat you warm?" Finally he adopted the practice of other doctors of billing a dollar for each phone consultation, which may have reduced the volume of calls.

When he could leave home, sometimes having to dig the car out of the snow and put chains on the wheels, he was off to his hospital visits, numerous in those pre-antibiotic days, and home visits. In the afternoon he held office hours in the building he and Dr. Amos Koontz owned at 1014 St. Paul Street. He usually sent his secretary, the faithful Charlotte Childs, out for his lunch— a grilled cheese sandwich or package of cheese and peanut butter crackers and a chocolate milkshake—not very healthy fare to combine with his constant smoking. After office hours there would be more home visits, especially to children too sick to come out or families with no transportation, thanks to gasoline rationing. Racing from Dundalk to a farm family with eight children in Ellicott City to the hospitals and everywhere in between, he would arrive home for a belated dinner at nine or ten. He figured he sometimes drove eighty miles a day on his rounds; as a physician he had a large gas ration and priority for new cars if they were available. Late at night he would pursue his reading and writing on endocrinology, before having a stiff nightcap and turning in. Sometimes late at night I would hear the phone ring, my mother rouse him, his feet hit the floor and soon he would be off on another emergency call.

This could not have been an easy regimen for my mother but I never heard her complain. She had full responsibility for the house, (with Mary Johnson now working in a parachute factory) the children's activities, and any social life there might be and always had a warm dinner and things running smoothly when he returned. She pitched in to Red Cross and hospital volunteer work.

In an interesting letter dated December 17, 1943, Lawson explained why he could not accept an offer from Dr. Edward Park, Chief of Pediatrics, to take an academic position in the Hopkins Medical School.

"December 17, 1943

Dr, Edwards A. Park
Harriet Lane Home
The Johns Hopkins Hospital
Baltimore, Maryland

Dear Doctor Park:

I am sorry to have been slow in replying to your nice letter about the teaching. I had hoped to tell you personally how complimented I felt, but it is hard for me to find time to see you at present.

For years I have found myself torn between the things I would like to do and those I have to do. You have put more enticing temptations in my way than anyone else. I would truly derive a great deal of satisfaction from teaching regularly and doing research intensively. I often dream of withdrawing some day from the hectic life I live and attempting to climb upon an academic pedestal, but by that time I shall probably be decrepit and seedy. At present I believe that whatever training and talents that I may have make the practice of pediatrics my first duty. Wartime conditions are such that everyone of us has to work his very hardest to meet the acute needs of the present, and even then people are being neglected.

The character of pediatric practice is such that it admits of practically no planning or arranging in advance. Unless one is able to withdraw to purely consulting or academic work, practice has to been given first and constant precedence over everything else in the twenty-four hours. Fortunately, I have been able to carry on my endocrine work with Dr. Fleischmann's help by squeezing it in during the day where it could fit, and by doing a large portion of it at night, on vacation, etc., but this has been more and more difficult since the war began. To set regular hours for a teaching program or other routine duties is about impossible. In the past few weeks the grippe epidemic (with a high incidence of otitis media, convulsions, etc.) has made the shortage of doctors very apparent and has kept me hopping without a pause from early morning until late at night.

I have a very guilty feeling about holding a title in the department when I do not enter more into teaching and other routine work, and wonder whether I should not give up such a title. I realize very well the needs of the pediatric department, and I know full well that you all are carrying double burdens during the war. I wish I could help more, and I would enjoy it. Nevertheless, I feel certain that I am needed still more in the daily drive of outside practice. I do want to carry on to the best of my abilities in the endocrine work and would like to give a great deal more time to it than I do. Sometime, if a let-up ever comes, I would like to give a whole course of endocrine lectures to the Staff — but a decent let-up never seems to come.

Dr. Fleischmann and I had hoped very much to chat with you at leisure about various phases of our work and to ask to have you thoughts and advice on many problems. I had planned to ask you and Dr. Fleischmann to have dinner with me at the Hopkins Club, so that we might spend an evening in discussion. This plan has been interrupted by the sudden onset of the grippe epidemic (which usually postpones my dinner to 10 P.M.). As soon as there is a let-up, perhaps we can arrange it.

Yours sincerely,

Lawson Wilkins"

13

SKIPPY'S DEATH

Saturday, January 15, 1944, was a dreary, sleety day. I was reading in bed, suffering from a sore throat, when I heard the front door slam. Then I heard voices making an unfamiliar sound. Were they laughing wildly? In a few minutes, Dad came to my room and told me that Skippy, aged sixteen, had been killed in a crash. The shock of seeing him cry uncontrollably was horrendous and made me realize that my parents could not always protect me or make things right. Our lives were drastically changed from that day on.

Because of the wartime shortage of laborers, Skip had had part-time and summer jobs since he was fourteen. He worked in the fields of a nursery. A tall, handsome, self-assured boy, he was popular and dated older girls who asked him to dances and parties because the older men were away in the army

He had a girlfriend two years older than he who was at college in Virginia. When he got his driver's license in September of 1943, he landed a job driving a mail truck for the post office. He was a junior at Friends, played varsity football and was vice president of the student council. He worked for the post office during the Christmas rush and was asked to stay on for weekends, leaving home before I was up. The old mail

Figure 8, George Lawson Wilkins II ("Skippy") 1927-1944

trucks were tall and top-heavy, resembling World War I ambulances. I never learned all the details of the accident but he struck a car, the truck turned over and he was dead on arrival at the emergency room of Union Memorial Hospital. My father who was seeing patients there was called to the emergency room to identify him. Then he had to drive home alone to tell my mother and me.

Because of wartime gas shortages, it was decided to hold Skip's funeral at home, instead of a church or funeral home. He was laid out in the dining room and for days there were streams of friends and relatives, condoling with us, bringing special foods, scarce in wartime, and flowers. It was a terrible, devastated time. In retrospect, I realize this time of expressing and sharing grief was the best way my parents could have endured the loss. My father always said that it was my mother's love and strength that made it possible for him to bear it. They were very wise in allowing me, aged twelve, to participate but sheltering me also.

Many family routines were changed. For several years we did not vacation on the Severn but went to friends in Rehoboth and Aunt Emilie's cottage on Lake Memphremagog in Vermont and toured New England and Quebec. Christmas was spent at Aunt Emilie's in Bethlehem, Pennsylvania, where the sounds of carols sung in the Moravian church in German (as he had learned many of them as a child) reduced my father to uncontrollable sobs.

My parents took up new activities. Lawson went back to carpentry learned in his childhood and redesigned and paneled our living room, replacing the Mission-style mantel piece with a graceful colonial one and building bookcases. He built a charming Sheraton-style serving table. His gardening became even more strenuous, including designing and laying a flagstone terrace; the garden that had been like a cement parking lot when the previous owners (and their nine children) moved out, became a showplace, requiring trips to York, Pennsylvania, for special perennials. My mother acquired a fine Knabe grand piano from the estate of a very musical man and made more time to play. This was the era when, by chance, I took up the viola with the school orchestra, inspiring Lawson to renew his acquaintance with the violin. Any friend or neighbor who played an instrument was dragooned into joining our musicales. It was a good thing that our neighborhood had large yards where the sound could dissipate.

About two years after Skip's death, Dr. Park's successor, Dr. Francis Schwentker, offered my father a full-time position to carry out Pediatric Endocrinology. With the doctors back from the war, Lawson felt free to follow his passion for research. He also felt exhausted by the stressful war years and was willing to accept a lower income to go full time. My mother, too, was delighted as she felt that pace would kill him and she was frequently very anxious when he was late coming home from his rounds of visits. Best of all, he was able to spend more time with her and me.

14

BEGINNING TO REAP THE REWARDS OF HIS LABORS

My parents began to travel, attending medical meetings in other parts of the country and Canada.

I do not know who the first of Lawson's fellows was. In 1947 or 1948, Salvador de Majo, who had left Argentina because of the Peron dictatorship, came to work with him. This quiet, gentle doctor was welcomed into family gatherings, subjected to the music, trips to the Severn and Maryland Hunt Cup, when my mother would polish her college Spanish; he remained a lifelong friend.

If Dad had any hopes of my heading into medicine (unlikely), they were not to come true. He took great pride in the fact that I did quite well at Roland Park Country School, getting good marks in the required biology and chemistry courses, but I never felt drawn to or thrilled by them. The sciences were the one weak area at the school and the way they were presented made them seem pretty incomprehensible to me. (The textbook for my introductory college biology course he also declared to be much too detailed and inappropriate.) If I had a strong drive to go into medicine I expect he would have supported me. He pointed out Harriet Guild, Helen Taussig, (bright lights at Hopkins), Mary Goodwin, Jean Stifler (practicing pediatricians) and Lydia Edwards, (researcher in mycobacteria who had an eminent career at NIH, UNRRHA and WHO) as wonderful role models, but always stressed what a hard profession it was for women. My mother steered me away from nursing with tales of bedpans and the servitude nursing students endured. Both parents encouraged me to volunteer at Hopkins Hospital, where I spent some high school summers running an antiquated cash register in the hectic Harriet Lane clinics, fetching charts and getting exposed to the variety of life there.

Lawson's enthusiasm for his work entered all aspects of his life; he enjoyed explaining it to my mother and me at the dinner table. When I asked him in my early teens how to explain it to my schoolmates, he said, "Just tell them I'm a big sex man." At thirteen I had bred a litter of Persian kittens to sell. Saturday night before an ad was to appear in *The Baltimore Sun*, he gathered Dr. Richard TeLinde, Chief of Gynecology and Dr. Frank Ford, Chief of Neurology, and other eminences around the table after dinner to determine the sex of the kittens. All four kittens were misdiagnosed, and when they were returned I had to refund the money paid for them; I did not earn enough to repay my parents the breeder's fee.

When it came time for college, my parents would have liked to have me near home at Goucher but realized I was ready to stretch my wings further. RPCS programmed as many students as possible to go to Wellesley, but, after thirteen years of sheltered female education, I chose Swarthmore. My father, who hated cold weather and felt somewhat depressed in winter, had dropped hints about the misery of New England weather and the dangers of winter sports (just look at Dr. TeLinde, who limped from a hip broken years before figure skating!) My parents were delighted to have me just outside Philadelphia, and were impressed with the academic atmosphere but, when they met some of the guys I went out with and realized how liberal the college was (this was the McCarthy era!), began to suggest that it would be nice if I would finish up at Goucher and meet more nice Baltimore boys. Considering their loss five years before, I have always appreciated that they resisted the urge to shelter me more than they did.

My parents usually planned a big party, with singing, around Christmas, when I was home from college, which included his fellows and house staff members he thought congenial. It was here I met Drs. John Crigler, David Smith, Alfred Bongiovanni, Gordon Kennedy, George Clayton, Jud Van Wyk, Mel Grumbach and many others but do not recall who worked with Lawson in which years. Later I came to know practically all the fellows he had and was impressed with what a brilliant and lively group they were. He loved them all, as surrogate sons, and delighted in their successes. I could feel the love they reciprocated for him.

15

1950

One fellow whose arrival I recall vividly was Claude Migeon. Lawson had decided to attend the first International Congress of Pediatrics in Zurich in the summer of 1950. After the difficult events of the 1940s, with Europe in recovery and feeling a little more affluent than before, Lawson found this a good opportunity to take my mother and me to Europe. I had just finished my first year at college. He meticulously researched and planned every detail of the trip and treated himself to his first thirty-five millimeter camera. The trip included England, Wales, Holland, France, Switzerland and a bit of Germany

Claude had been in touch with Lawson and came to meet with him at the Hotel de Paris. My mother and I met him in the lobby as we were on our way out. Meeting a Parisian (for the present), and recalling highlights of her 1923 visit to Paris, she sought his opinion on where to shop for kid gloves and perfume. I do not recall Claude's answer but I remember his flabbergasted expression. Then my father asked if Claude thought it would be appropriate to take his eighteen-year-old daughter to the Folies Bergères. Claude hesitated and then said, "Well, my grandmother took me when I was five." I do not remember what we did with this

Figure 9. Lawson, Lucile and Betsy
Wilkins, The Hague, 1950

information but we were all delighted when it was arranged for Claude to come to Baltimore, and he became a lifelong friend.

Another memorable highlight of the trip was our stay in Brittany, which Dad had visited when he was stationed in St. Nazaire. We stayed in the ancient walled town of Vannes where his memories became ever more colorful, especially one of a picnic he went on with the daughters of a baker. He spied a bakery he was sure was the one and we trooped in. He told the middle-aged ladies who ran it that he was one of the young soldiers they had taken on a picnic at Chateau Suscinio thirty-three years before. He took many pictures of all of us smiling outside the bakery. When the pictures were developed back in Baltimore, revealing two rather plump ladies of unexceptional appearance, he said they had indeed aged—"But you should have seen their beautiful cousin who was visiting from Paris!" I don't know what the ladies made of the experience.

The highlight of the trip was the ten to fourteen-day stay in Zurich. I had never been to such a Congress. After the deprivations and isolation of war, the atmosphere was thrilling as this great number of scientists were able to meet one another and share their ideas. Lawson was very excited about the results he had had treating patients with cortisone, just recently available, and had a large display with many pictures and charts for the poster sessions. My mother and I had been enlisted in the early summer to help arrange the panels on the living room floor and packing and transporting them had been quite a job. The results exceeded Lawson's wildest expectations as he became friendly with many international colleagues and was approached by the publisher, Charles C. Thomas, who asked him to write a textbook of Pediatric Endocrinology.

Back at home Lawson worked on the book with his usual intensity and it came out in record time; my mother and I spent hours with cards on the floor creating the index.

During subsequent summers of my college years, when I felt I should seek jobs to help with college expenses, Lawson found ways to direct my interests. One summer while my parents were on a professional trip, they arranged for me to share our house with John and Joan Hampson, psychiatrists he had brought onto his team to deal with the psychological aspects of patient care, which he recognized were beyond his abilities. When I was planning to take an unexciting job in a secretarial pool, he inveigled a more interesting position for me as a case aide in the social service department at the hospital. (Although his sister had some frightful experiences in her career as a social worker in various cities, he felt this was definitely an acceptable profession for me.) This summer job led to my accepting a job as a case aide at the hospital for a year after my graduation in 1953.

Living at home for a year after college and carpooling to work with my father was pleasant but I found the job limited and the atmosphere of Baltimore stifling. To continue in social work I must get a master's degree and decided to go to Columbia, sharing an apartment in New York with my best friend from Baltimore. In the summer of 1954, before starting in school again, I took a three-month trip in Europe with a college friend, Susan Harvey. Lawson was a visiting professor at Guys Hospital, London, and my parents were ensconced in a tiny, charming eighteenth-century house. Susan and I made that the base for travels in England, sometimes with my parents who took us to nicer places than we could afford on our shoestring budgets. Susan and I had a grand time in Cambridge with Gordon and Minnie Kennedy and their children; Gordon had worked in Lawson's department, sharing a miserable, hot apartment on Broadway with Claude. In Holland we visited Janny van Walbeek Kleyn, a hearty, fun-loving pediatric cardiologist whom we had met in 1950 when she worked with Dr. Helen Taussig, the renowned pediatric cardiologist who collaborated with Dr. Albert Blalock at Hopkins on the development of the operation to cure "blue babies." In Copenhagen my parents joined us for a busy, fun-filled week with Henning and Else Andersen. Henning, who had spent six months or so working with Lawson's pediatric endocrine group, had taken a week's vacation to entertain Lawson. Vacationing friends of theirs lent us their house. The Andersens' sons were away at camp and Henning packed the week with merriment. When our energies would flag and we would suggest going back to the house to rest or sleep, he would decree that it was time to go to Tivoli; his favorite place was the Mysteriske Hus, a mirrored set of rooms where everything and everyone looked crazy. He would laugh so uproariously that we would become weak with laughter; the Danes certainly know how to enjoy life! In Copenhagen we also spent time with Lawson's old friend, Lydia Edwards, now a pediatrician with WHO studying mycobacteria. In Paris we were entertained, also, by some of my father's colleagues and had one memorable evening around a dinner table with one family, sharply divided over France's policy in pulling out of Indo-China—a foretaste of what we were to experience with the US policy in the sixties. After that, Susan and I went merrily off on our own through France, Germany and Italy, leaving my parents in London without word of us for six weeks, suffering alternately from rage and anxiety.

After getting my MSW I stayed on to work in an excellent social service department at the New York Hospital. I took a position working with previously undiagnosed tuberculosis patients with far advanced disease with lung cavitation. This was a very interesting group of patients, often with deep psychological problems, who had long hospitalizations while they were being treated experimentally with ioniazid. My father was very worried about me being exposed to TB and insisted that I should be inoculated with BCG. This had been used in Great Britain without any proof that it provided protection. As it turned one's tuberculin test from negative to positive, the researchers with whom I worked strongly opposed my taking it and losing a means of learning if I contracted TB. My father was so worried and wanted to get any protection he could for me that I gave in and had the shot, to the annoyance of the "TB researchers."

Those were exhilarating, fun-filled years. I relished using social work skills with patients struggling with illness, I enjoyed all that New York had to offer and felt I was meeting more interesting people in a week than in a year in Baltimore. I went home for holidays and my parents included me in parties and hoped I would find potential dates. They worried about me in the wilds of New York; each only visited me once in four years there, preferring not to think about the dangers of the city. Also, they were having a great time with travels connected with Dad's increasing fame.

16

TRIP TO SOUTH AMERICA

In November of 1957 Lawson was invited to an international conference in Buenos Aires, first class, all expenses paid for him and Lucile. Invitations also came from Brazil, Uruguay, Chile and Peru. For this once-in-a-lifetime trip, I persuaded my boss to let me take two years' vacation back-to-back and my parents to let me join them; I contributed for my fares and some expenses. It was a fabulous month as we were lavishly entertained wherever we went. In Buenos Aires we renewed acquaintance with Dr. Salvador de Majo who had left Argentina during the Peron dictatorship and worked with my father. We first met Dr. Cesar Bergada who later came to work with the endocrine group, bringing his lovely wife, Estela, six children and fabulous piano skills that enlivened many evenings. Dr. Jose Cara was an old friend in Cordoba who, like Salvador de Majo, had come to work with Lawson's group during the worst of the Peron dictatorship. He and his wife, Maria, took us traveling in the Cordoba region. In every city, Lawson gave talks and early morning rounds before the sightseeing and entertainments began, ending with elegant dinners at late, Latin hours. In Lima we did not sit down to dinner until midnight, but still Dr. Nicanor Carmona picked Lawson up for rounds at seven the next morning. Fortunately, Lawson had been accustomed to such a schedule before and took advantage of the universal siesta.

17

BETSY'S MARRIAGE

My parents had tried to mask their anxiety over whether and whom I might marry but they could not hide their delight when I became engaged to Philip McMaster. Although Phil had graduated from Hopkins Medical School and we had many mutual friends, we met not in Baltimore but at the New York Hospital where he was an intern. When we visited my parents on weekends, Lawson so enjoyed his company that he had to be reminded that Phil was here to see me and we might have plans to go out. When he very properly came to "ask for my hand" Lawson got so wrapped up in talking with him, that my mother and I had to linger in the kitchen for an hour, till we finally barged into the living room to remind them of the purpose of the visit.

Everything about Phil suited my parents, as well as me. He was now working at the NIH in immunology research, uncertain whether he would stay in research or go into practice. His father was a well-known scientist, one of the first members of the Rockefeller Institute. His family played the same kind of charades and sang the same kind of music as we did, as well as being lifelong sailors. His father even played the violin, self-taught, but much more in key than Lawson.

My mother wanted to plan a June wedding but we insisted that we wanted to get married in December of 1958. My parents pulled out all the stops and Lu had a great time planning the wedding and reception, a joyous occasion for us all. She looked radiantly beautiful in an electric blue silk faille dress (Figures 10, 11, 12, 13).

Figure 10. Wedding of Elizabeth Biays
Wilkins and Dr. Philip Robert Bache
McMaster December 13, 1958,

Figure 11. Wedding of Elizabeth Biays
Wilkins and Dr. Philip Robert Bache
McMaster December 13, 1958,

Figure 12. Wedding of Elizabeth Biays
Wilkins and Dr. Philip Robert Bache
McMaster December 13, 1958,

Figure 13. Wedding of Elizabeth Biays
Wilkins and Dr. Philip Robert Bache
McMaster December 13, 1958

18

LUCILE'S DEATH

Sometime in the first week of May 1959, my father called me to say he was taking my mother to the hospital, as Lu had had a seizure and symptoms that he thought indicated a subdural hematoma. My heart sank with dread immediately and I strongly suspected the worst. Lawson remained in denial for a remarkably long time and could never bring himself to talk openly with Lu; they each kept up a pretense to protect the other. She died in a coma on June 10. Phil and I were so glad we had insisted on the earlier wedding date and given her so much happiness.

Even before Lu died, Lawson said he could never live alone; he would have to remarry. Following her death he was deeply despondent, having at least two auto crashes that took him to the hospital and exhausting some of his dearest friends with his outpouring of grief. As with Skip's death, he personally wrote long responses to the hundreds of letters that poured in from all over the world. Not only had he lost Lu, but being sixty-five, he was required to step down from his position as head of the department. He was glad to turn it over to Drs. Migeon and Blizzard and would continue to work, write and lecture, but he felt doubly bereaved. I was torn between his constant neediness in Baltimore and getting settled in my own marriage and home in Bethesda.

19

REMARRIAGE

In September of 1960 Phil and I moved to Paris where he was to spend two years in research in immunochemistry at the Pasteur Institute. For me this was heaven and Lawson promised to visit us. Claude and Barbara Migeon, recently married, devoted immense amounts of time, energy and love to alleviating Lawson's loneliness. They even let him come on their honeymoon, attending conferences in Scotland and Denmark together! After arriving in Paris, I received an international call (a rarity in those days) from Claude, informing me Lawson had had a coronary. He had told Claude to tell me not to come as he was in good hands and doing well. Very soon I received a letter in which he told me that he was engaged to Catrina Anderson Francis, called "Teence," the sister of his lawyer, an old friend. They had a small wedding before a justice of the peace and visited us on their honeymoon in April, 1961. His happiness was infectious. We had a very merry time showing them our favorite haunts, introducing them to some of our friends and allowing ourselves to be taken to some fabulous restaurants. On a restricted diet following his coronary, Lawson would accept only two ladles full of rich sauce instead of three and was trying to stop smoking. He and Teence had some wonderful trips in the next two years.

20

LAWSON'S DEATH

In the year following our return from France, Phil and I saw a great deal of Lawson and Teence; he was eagerly awaiting the birth of our first child. On September 27, 1963, Teence called us to come see him in the hospital; he had suffered another coronary. We were in time to tell him how much we loved him. He was very weak and tired, kept alive only by extreme measures. He died that day. Our son, Charles, was born November 2. Over the years I have come to recognize more and more how blessed I was to have had such a brilliant, original, highly principled, generous, loving and funny father, and a lovely mother who, with her warmth, graciousness, wide cultural interests, and devotion and loyalty to family and friends, perfectly complemented her husband and made it possible for him to achieve great things. It is a tragic lack that Phil's and my children never knew these two wonderful people who longed so for grandchildren, but we are all immeasurably proud of their accomplishments in the wider world.

21

AFTERWORD

In his chapters, Claude Migeon has described with great sensitivity his fondness for my father. I know that Claude filled a special place in Lawson's life, both as a brilliant colleague and as a surrogate son. I cannot fully express my gratitude to Claude and Barbara for all they did for him, in the happier times, in his lonely, despondent days and in his illnesses. They supported him when Phil and I were not there and when some of his closest friends could not endure his grief. And how many newlyweds let the boss join them on their honeymoon?

It is hard to believe that Claude and Lawson only knew each other for thirteen years. I have now known Claude and Barbara for fifty years longer. They knew my father better than anyone else alive and have become like family to me. I am so grateful that they have pushed this book to completion. They have my deep appreciation and love.

22

ACKNOWLEDGMENTS

Editing and technical assistance generously provided by Joseph Philip Duryee McMaster.

23

REFERENCES

1. Pitrof, Larry. Dean's Office. University of Maryland Medical School, Baltimore, Maryland. Personal Communication, 2004.
2. Baltimore Sun, The Miscellaneous clippings
3. Bongiovanni, Alfred M. Presentation of the John Howland Medal and Award of the American Pediatric Society to Dr. Lawson Wilkins. Reprinted from the Journal of Pediatrics, St. Louis. Vol. 63, No. 4, Part 2, Pages 803-807; 808-811, October, 1963.
4. Esslinger, Dean R. Friends for 200 Years, A History of Baltimore's Oldest school. Baltimore Friends School in Cooperation with the Museum and Library of the Maryland Historical Society. Baltimore, 1983.
5. Morley, Felix. For the Record. Regnery, Gateway Inc. South Bend, Indiana. 1979.
6. Harvey, A. McGehee, Brieger, Gert H., Abrams, Susan L., and McKusick, Victor A. A Model of Its Kind: Vol. I. A Centennial History of Medical History at Johns Hopkins, 1983.
7. Base Hospital 18 Association, History of Base Hospital No. 18. Thomsen, Ellis Co. Baltimore, New York, 1919.
8. Weiner, Ruth Fleischmann. Personal correspondence, 2013

LAWSON WILKINS
AND MY LIFE

Claude J. Migeon, MD

ACKNOWLEDGEMENTS

The individuals who have helped with this work are numerous.

I have included comments of Dr. Hugh Morgan (Chapter 40) and Dr. John Eager Howard, a great friend and physician of Wilkins (Chapter 41).

I have also obtained some writing from the fellows, including John Crigler (Chapter 13), Judson Van Wyk (Chapter 56), Melvin Grumbach, Robert Blizzard and John Money (Chapter 57). My wife, Barbara Migeon, was close to Lawson and her comments are included in chapters 47, 48 and 49. The proof-reading has been made by Betsy McMaster, Barbara Migeon, Jack Fuqua and Arlan Rosenbloom. They should be thanked greatly.

Michael Wong, a graduate of Johns Hopkins University in 2013, has been extremely helpful in formatting the manuscript. Michael's long-range goal is medical school.

Most importantly, the efforts of Dr Jack Fuqua and Dr. Jacques Migeon as editors have made the publication of this book possible.

Finally, I should mention the financial assistance of Genentech and the most generous gift of Dr. Nadia Zerhouni and her husband, Elias.

To all these people and those who I have forgotten to name, I am extremely thankful for their thoughtfulness.

ADDITIONAL NOTE

For several years, funds had been collected from past fellows and friends of Lawson Wilkins. With the help of Dr. George Dover, the Lawson Wilkins Professorship of Pediatric Endocrinology was established. The inaugural recipient was Dr. Sally Radovick on December 6, 2006.

CHAPTER TWO

TABLE OF CONTENTS

1

INTRODUCTION

From the first day we met, in 1950, I addressed you as Dr. Wilkins. This of course was a mark of respect that is characteristic of the European culture. In later years, some of the fellows of my age or even younger called you Lawson; I never could do this because of the enormous respect I always had for you. Even when I came to see you at Hopkins on the last day of your life, I asked, "How are you doing, Dr. Wilkins?" I hope that you will understand that it is out of respect and not lack of affection if I continue in this chapter to address you as Dr. Wilkins.

Clearly this memoir is about you, Dr. Wilkins, but starting in 1950, you have played such a major role at the most important junctions of my life that it is hard for me to separate my life from yours. First in 1950, you were willing to bring me to the Johns Hopkins Hospital. Then in 1952, when I had to make a decision on what to do next after two years of fellowship, you convinced me not only that I should come back to the United States but also that I should enlarge my field of knowledge by going to another center in order to learn more basic science. For that purpose you wrote to many of your friends about available post-doctoral fellowships and helped me choose among them. This is when I went to work at the University of Utah in Salt Lake City. In 1955, when I was ready to leave Salt Lake City and was planning to join John Crigler in Boston at the Children's Hospital, you gave me a call along with a letter asking me to come back to Baltimore as an assistant professor. And, of course, I did. In the following years after my return to Baltimore, you hinted on many occasions about my getting married. You even made some suggestions. Eventually, when I married Barbara in 1960, you were one of the wedding party of five. Later when I considered moving to the University of Florida in Gainesville, you asked Bill Thomas to give you a little time to figure out how you could keep me in Baltimore. And there again I did what you suggested. So I usually find it difficult to talk about Lawson Wilkins without recounting my life and career.

2

UNIVERSITY OF PARIS, SCHOOL OF MEDICINE (1949)

My eagerness to visit the United States initially arose from a rich personal experience.

In 1949, there was only one medical school in Paris, the University of Paris. However, the clinical clerkships could be taken in all the hospitals around the city. I chose the Hopital des Enfants Malades in Necker. There, I worked with Professor Julien Huber and Professor Sotirios Briskas. Indeed, I did my medical thesis in that department. Dr. Briskas had a sister in Chicago who had two sons and a daughter. During the Second World War, both sons were in the armed forces. Both of them came to France; the oldest was killed in the Battle of the Bulge in Bastogne. At the time of this battle, I was in Rethel (Ardennes) about fifty miles south of Bastogne. I could hear the deep rolling noise of the artillery and it was quite frightening.

His brother and sister, William and Stella Nanos, decided to visit their uncle in Paris and also to go to the grave of their brother who was in the large American Cemetery of Bastogne. Dr. Briskas had asked me to help entertain them. We eventually visited their brother's grave. We drove there with my family. This was a powerfully emotional experience for them and for me. Of course it brought us closer together and during their nine months in Paris, we were extremely close. The day they left was a sad day for all of us and we promised to see each other again in the future.

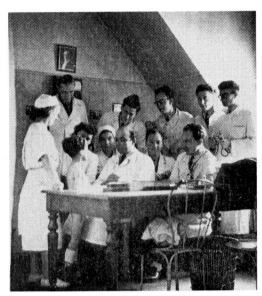

Figure 14. The "consultation externe" at
the Hopital des Enfants Malades. (1948)

This is how the idea came to me that I should try to obtain a fellowship in the United States. I applied at various institutions. In addition to my medical studies, I had obtained certificates in chemistry and biochemistry. As part of this work, I had done some research about the effects of copper on metabolism of rats. Having seen a flyer on the bulletin board at the School of Medicine, I applied for and received a Fulbright Fellowship. However, this fellowship did not require that I have a specific place to work. During my interview, I suggested Chicago would be a good place to work. However, somehow with my background and with my clinical interest I was assigned to the Pediatric Endocrine Clinic of Dr. Lawson Wilkins at The Johns Hopkins Hospital.

I was extremely pleased with this assignment, although I would have preferred to be in Chicago closer to my friends. When I told Bill and Stella of the location for my fellowship, they suggested I could easily visit them at vacation times.

My knowledge of geography was quite good, and I could envision Washington, Philadelphia and Boston on the East Coast of the United States, but I did not know where Baltimore was located, until I consulted an atlas and learned that Baltimore was very close to Washington, DC.

3

IN PARIS (SPRING 1950)

I received an official typewritten letter from Baltimore, signed by Lawson Wilkins. I was quite pleased. In my clinic at the Enfants Malades, I had seen patients with Turner Syndrome and had read papers written by Wilkins. I never learned why I was accepted. My medical thesis was entitled: "L'ossification: influences endocriniennes. Importance en thérapeutique infantile." The thesis even got a silver medal! Dr. Wilkins must have thought that I was interested in learning more about the endocrine effects on bone growth. He had an NIH grant titled "Relationship of hormones on growth and development." (AM-00180). In his letter, Dr. Wilkins announced that he was going to be in Paris, stopping on his way to the Sixth International Congress of Pediatrics, which was going to take place in Zurich, Switzerland. In addition, Dr. Wilkins asked to meet with me, if possible, at his hotel.

Needless to say, I was excited as well as nervous about this first encounter with Dr. Wilkins. I'm not quite sure that I knew what to expect but for some reason, despite the letter of acceptance, I had the feeling it was going to be a test that might influence whether I really got a fellowship and the position.

4

MEETING THE WILKINS FAMILY

On the chosen day, I took the subway from the hospital to the hotel where the Wilkinses were staying. I must have been a bit late because, when I arrived to the hotel, there were three people lined up waiting for me on the sidewalk, starting from the right, Dr. Wilkins, and then Mrs. Wilkins and their teenage daughter, Betsy. (Figure 9) Perhaps because they were standing on the sidewalk and I was at the level of the street, they appeared to me to be quite tall. Later, I realized they were average height. Dr. Wilkins wore his usual gray charcoal black suit with a button-down blue shirt and a dark blue tie. He looked intimidating to me, a cigarette in his right hand. Mrs. Wilkins was quite elegant and very fashionable. And then there was a teenage girl, who was introduced by Dr. Wilkins as his daughter, Betsy. She appeared to be a young lady who knew the world. On the other hand, I felt rather ignorant of the proper manners for such encounters.

Dr. Wilkins directed the flow of questions, but I have to admit I did not always understand what he said, because at this time in my life, I certainly didn't have a deep knowledge of the English language. I'm not sure if Dr. Wilkins said that he was accepting me or was pleased to meet me, it was not clear what he said.

Eventually, I understood a very specific question from Mrs. Wilkins: where could she purchase gloves? I believe that she added that France was well-known for the quality of gloves and that she was anxious to find a place to buy such gloves. I have to admit I had no idea where she should go to find gloves. My own gloves were bought by my mother, and I had no idea where she purchased them. So, I had to say that I was sorry I did not know. I really felt terrible, and so incompetent, not knowing where somebody coming from the United States could find the best quality French gloves.

I believe the next question was from Dr. Wilkins, asking me where there was a good restaurant that would not be too expensive. I believe that is what he asked. As a medical student I was not very affluent. Toward the end of medical school and before passing the final thesis, one can replace a vacationing physician at least for a summer. I had done that a few times. This was my source of revenue for the rest of the year. I was also in the business of giving intravenous injections as a treatment for venereal disease to foreigners in their hotel rooms, per orders of Dr. Briskas. It seemed to me that most of them needed therapy because they had a positive syphilis test. Penicillin was not "invented" yet, and intravenous arsenic therapy was the treatment of choice. Neither of these activities made me very rich and I certainly never went to restaurants. So, during this interview I felt trapped for a second time, unable to answer questions of interest to the Wilkins family. I remember breaking into a cold sweat, believing that I had totally blown my chances of being accepted by Dr. Wilkins for my fellowship. Reaching very deep in my memory, I retrieved the name of a restaurant. Although I had never eaten there, I said "Well, maybe Le Grand Vefour." I remembered that name because it was unusual, but I didn't know that it was, indeed, a high-class restaurant, which certainly was very expensive. I doubt that the Wilkins family ever went there, and I never returned to this conversation to find out.

By that time, I had the feeling that the two ladies, aware of my anxiety and feelings of incompetence, decided to return toward the entrance of the hotel. Dr. Wilkins tried to tell me that he was going to make an important presentation in Zurich. Our only difficulty was that we were having a two-way conversation, he not understanding too well what I said in poor English, and I being able to understand only parts of his comments. After a few minutes of this futile exercise, we said goodbye. I went away from our encounter totally deconstructed, as the philosophers would say. Shaking hands with Dr. Wilkins, I was miserable, feeling that I had ruined my chances of going to the United States. I went to a bistro and asked for a café creme. Feeling terribly cold inside,

I don't know if it was the weather or the remnants of that cold sweat. I was so unhappy about my inadequate performance.

Betsy McMaster has also written about this encounter and the question of whether Dr. Wilkins could bring his daughter to the Folies Bergères. I do not have a clear memory of this part of the conversation. However, I have to state that Betsy greatly exaggerated my early age going to this spectacle. I was not five years old; actually I was six. My parents had bought tickets for the Promenade (the space behind the boxes, where you must stand up to see the show). The trouble with the Promenade is that it is separated from the boxes by a tall wooden partition. My father had to lift me to see the stage. But when we noticed that a box was empty, I sneaked down there and had the best possible seat; I very much enjoyed the show!

5

JUNE-JULY 1950

Despite my first catastrophic interview with Dr. Wilkins, I continued to fill out a number of papers that were requested for the actual fellowship application. I obtained letters of recommendation from my clinical chiefs, Drs. Julien Huber and Sotirios Briskas, and Professor Michel Polonovski who was head of the Department of Biochemistry at the medical school, with whom I had been doing some research during the previous two years.

At the same time I had to finish putting together my medical thesis. The text had been typed by a secretary and figures had been made to go along with the text. All this material had to be assembled and a total of fifteen copies of the thesis had to be delivered to Ecole de Médecine.

In addition, not knowing whether I was actually going to obtain a fellowship, I had to make plans for my financial support. I had made arrangements to go to Lievin in the Pas-de-Calais (my actual birthplace), where I would stand-in for a vacationing pediatrician from June 30 to August 3.

During that time I was too busy with patients to think about my fellowship with Dr. Wilkins.

6

ON TO JOHNS HOPKINS HOSPITAL! (AUGUST 1950)

When I came back to Paris on August 4 there was a letter asking me to appear at the Service Universitaire des Relations avec l'Etranger, 55 Rue St. Dominique on August 9 at 2:00 p.m. This interview went well, even though it was carried out in English. I was told to see Mademoiselle Papillon (no joke!) on Saturday the twelfth to apply for my passport and US visa. While picking up my passport on Friday the eighteenth, I met a young lady, Mademoiselle Nadine Gregouroff, who was also an applicant for a Fulbright Fellowship. We tried to reassure each other about this great adventure that we were embarking on. She mentioned that she had met a few other French students who were also going. She had an appointment at the American embassy for her visa on the twenty-fourth of August. Mine was the next day, on the twenty-fifth. I met with Mr. Holt at the American embassy who carried out all the appropriate formalities and gave me my visa. Mr. Holt was very kind. He explained that after arriving in New York, I would go to Washington, DC, where I would spend four weeks getting accustomed to the American way of life and to the language (someone had probably noted my poor English). Then, I would take the train to Baltimore.

Finally he told me that my boat would depart on August thirty-first, six days later. Mr. Holt stated that he hoped the visit would be educational and profitable. At the door of his office, he shook my hand, gave me a pat on the back, wishing me a good trip - Bon Voyage - and good luck.

7

THE TRIP TO THE UNITED STATES OF AMERICA

A bruptly, it dawned on me that I was really departing for a long trip across the Atlantic and that I had to prepare for it. During the six days that remained, I had to go and get my tickets for the train and boat from a travel agency. I also had to obtain the addresses of my contacts in Washington, DC, and in Baltimore. This was a most stressful six days, saying goodbye to friends and family, finding a place to store my books and belongings. There was also the need to make a trip to the bank to determine my real worth. I knew that the end point was The Harriet Lane Home. To go to a "home" seemed quite propitious to me. The French people think of "home" as a "homey place" with a congenial environment. At that time, I did not know the full name of the Department of Pediatrics at Johns Hopkins Hospital: The Harriet Lane Home for Invalid Children.

Thursday, August 31, 1950: that was "Departing Day." I had to be at the station at 9:22 a.m. for a train to Le Havre. It arrived at noon. I carried a large suitcase and a raincoat full of hope in the pockets. When I arrived in Le Havre, my family had driven there with my brother, Michel, and sister, Claudine, all of them saying goodbye and shedding a few tears. I boarded the boat and waved goodbye to France. It was certainly a very poignant moment when I saw my family disappearing slowly in the harbor as I was moving away from the pier. However, I cheered up after a few hours as I met the other Fulbright Fellows who were going to the States. Like me, they were sad to leave their families but also excited to go. We kept each other company, while discovering where each of us was going. One was headed for Philadelphia, another to Indiana and another to Seattle. One of them was to stay in New York. There was also a minister who was joining a religious school in the South. Needless to say, we tried to reassure each other and actually had a wonderful time discussing our past and our plans for the future. In those days, travel by boat was an adventure in itself. First we went to Southampton where we stopped for several hours, and nine days later on Saturday, September 9, we arrived in New York at 8:30 p.m. The view of the lighted Statue of Liberty was incredible. Because it was late, we could not disembark and we had to wait until the next morning, Sunday. Perhaps because we were a little bit scared of being on our own, we remained together all day Sunday. On Monday, we separated and headed off in our individual directions.

Figure 15. My aunt (adoptive mother) as I get ready to embark on the De Grasse at Le Havre. (August 30, 1950)

8

WASHINGTON, DC: PREPARING FOR JOHNS HOPKINS (SEPTEMBER 1950)

My orders were to go to Washington. At the address given to me, a secretary told me that I had a reservation in a boarding house on 1406 10th Street NW. All the other boarders were American; about fifteen of them. None were Fulbright Fellows. They were in Washington for a short period of training or study. During our suppers together they introduced me to a new way of life. When corn on the cob was served, as a well-educated Frenchman, I approached the cob with my fork and knife; somehow the cob slid off my plate and ended up in the middle of the dining table. That was good for a laugh! Dr. Wilkins also laughed when I told him about it and it became part of the repertoire of my misadventures. I also told him about my first experience with baseball. One night, the boarders encouraged me to go to the game with them. I explained that I was not familiar with baseball but the boarders assured me that they would teach me as the game progressed. Afterward, my perception was of long periods of inaction (eating hot dogs and drinking beer) interrupted by a few periods when all the spectators were standing, gesticulating and shouting. There was no need for explanation during the quiet periods and I could not get any explanation during the rare periods of exaltation.

Dr. Wilkins pointed out that many words of the baseball language were often used in everyday conversation. And so I learned about "a hit," "home plate," "home run," "first base" etc.

The days in Washington were quite busy and instructive. It was a wonderful experience with visits to museums, the Senate and the House, and the White House. And, of course, I saw all the great monuments, including the imposing statue of Lincoln and the Jefferson Memorial. There were also well-organized lectures on the pronunciation of the English language. I worked very hard at this, as I was anxious to make a better impression on Dr. Wilkins at our next encounter.

9

AT JOHNS HOPKINS HOSPITAL, UNDER THE DOME (OCTOBER 1950)

On Monday, October 9, I repacked my luggage and took a taxi to Union Station on my way to Baltimore. Another taxi took me from Penn Station to the Johns Hopkins Hospital. The driver deposited me at the entrance on Broadway and helped me with my luggage. As he turned to me, the driver must have noticed some doubt on my face. Pointing to the main entrance, he said, "This is it!" I looked at the Dome and the 19th-century main building with its two annexes. It looked quite old and old-fashioned rather than modern, as I expected. It was a terribly hot day, ninety degrees or more at noontime. I picked up my luggage, climbed the steps to the entrance of the hospital and was met by the doorman who looked at me with a somewhat suspicious eye, wondering where I was going with my large valise. I told him that I was going to the Harriet Lane Home. Certainly; he explained how to go there, but I did not understand everything he said. I moved inside, put my luggage down and raised my eyes to see the bigger-than-life statue of Jesus Christ in the entrance hall under the Dome. I sensed that he felt sorry for me; or was it that I felt sorry for myself? At least it

Figure 16. The Harriet Lane Home. (October 1950)

was cooler under the Dome. After some rest, I picked up my luggage again, moved around the big stairs, turned right in the corridor and then left—finally, arriving in a building that I was told was the Harriet Lane Home.

I was most disappointed; in my imagination, I had visualized a beautiful, pleasant "home." The first floor of the Harriet Lane was far from this: rather old, small, very busy. At noon, everybody seemed to rush around and talk very loudly. Somebody again asked me where I was going and I explained I was trying to find Dr. Wilkins. I was told to take the elevator and go to the fifth floor. The elevator was easy to locate. This was a big double-door of very shiny red copper. When the elevator came down, the two doors were opened by a "colored lady" (as it was politically correct to say then.) She helped me get my luggage into the elevator and told me that her name was Odessa. She was a wonderful young lady, always smiling. Her job was to open and close the two doors of the elevator, and once they were closed, to maneuver a lever to bring the elevator up or down. It was always a problem to stop exactly at the right level. Sometimes Odessa would miss the floor and would have to close the doors again and run the elevator down a little bit to make it just at the right level. We reached the fifth floor and again Odessa helped me with my luggage.

10

THE FIFTH FLOOR OF HARRIET LANE HOME

I guess I was getting tired by this time. Also I was overtaken by the heat as the fifth floor was directly under a flat roof. I had no means to check the temperature, but I suspect it was at least a hundred degrees. This fifth floor did not ease my disappointment with my new "Home." The corridors were cluttered; there were several cases of bottles of Coca-Cola, drums of organic solvents; some appeared full, others empty. There was a pile of serving trays on the floor. A small table near the elevator was holding a half dozen bottles containing yellow liquid—probably urine samples brought up from the clinical floors by a nurse.

Again someone asked me where I was going, and I explained that I wanted to find Dr. Wilkins. "Go to the end of the corridor and then turn right and you will find his office right there."

Straight ahead at the end of the corridor a door opened to an office with typewriters and secretaries. On the right, I found a narrow, short passageway; on one side, the wall was covered with shelves from the floor to the ceiling. Those shelves were loaded with jars of chemicals. I'm sure there were more than several hundred bottles sitting there, with all sorts of sodium and potassium salts, including potassium cyanide. And then I came to the office of Dr. Wilkins. I knocked at the door, which was actually open. He was sitting behind his desk, a cigarette in his hand. Noticing that I carried a big piece of luggage, he suggested that I leave it in the corridor as there was not that much space in his office. Indeed, besides two shelves with books, his chair on one side of his desk and my chair on the other, there was certainly no space for luggage. He welcomed me very warmly. With his very deep bass voice, he asked whether

I had had a good trip, and I, of course, returned the compliment, asking if he had a good visit in Switzerland. He reported that his exhibit in Zurich had been extremely well-received. He also explained that the exhibit was a summary of his book that had just been published (*The Diagnosis and Treatment of Endocrine Disorders in Childhood and Adolescence. First Edition. 1950*). He had received a few copies and he presented me with one of them that I could read it at my convenience. Dr. Wilkins took his pen and wrote on the front page: "To my good friend and colleague, Claude Migeon." Later, when I checked his writing, I was amazed and warmed deeply in my heart about the word "friend." I was also surprised and flattered to be referred to as the colleague of an American professor who had just written a textbook that was to become the "bible" of pediatric endocrinologists.

He also brought up the question of lodging. He told me that the House Staff had rooms in various places, some were in the building called "Main Residence," which was near the Wilmer Institute; others had rooms under the Dome and at the Nurses Home across the street on Broadway. At that point, Dr. Wilkins got up from his chair and took me to meet everyone and to visit the laboratories. The labs were certainly close to his office since they were just next door, at the end of the narrow corridor.

11

THE PEOPLE IN THE LABS OF PEDIATRIC ENDOCRINOLOGY AND THEIR CLOSE NEIGHBORS

As we entered through the door, someone stated that there was a lot of or-ganic solvents being used and to please keep the cigarettes out. Dr. Wilkins agreed, made two steps backward and kept his lighted cigarette behind his back, like a child caught smoking by his parents.

This first lab was a very large room with a working bench in the middle, each side of the bench being a working area. There were also benches on three sides of the room. The fourth side, on our left when we entered included a big fume hood and on the right was a large sink attended by a short black lady of about fifty years of age, Miss Virginia who prepared glassware. She was the first person I met in the lab; I was told that she was a wonderful lady who was most important to all the work of the lab as all the results depended on the cleanliness of the glassware. Miss Virginia was born and raised in the Johns Hopkins neighborhood. She had worked all her life at the hospital and was part of a group of African-Americans who labored in this institution and were thoroughly dedicated.

Then Dr. Wilkins introduced me to the two technicians, Henry Schulte and Mary Ellen Crafton. They said hello rather quickly as they were very busy with their work. The last person in the room was Dr. Lytt Gardner. Dr. Wilkins explained that Lytt was an assistant professor. He had just arrived from Boston where he had been working with Nathan Talbot, Edna Sobel, Fred Bartter, Jack Crawford and Ann Forbes. At that time, I did not know these investigators, but the fact that Dr. Gardner was coming from Harvard was impressive enough for me. After the busy and noisy laboratory, Dr. Wilkins showed me two little rooms that were located on the other side of the galleries of chemicals. In the first one we stowed my luggage. In the other small room was a huge instrument taking almost all the space, and a young tall man, Dr. John Crigler. At that point, Dr. Wilkins told me that this instrument, a flame photometer, was the last word in electrolyte measurement. This was most important in the study of electrolyte balances in the children with salt-losing adrenal hyperplasia. I was also told that John had just finished his year as Chief Resident at Harriet Lane and that now he was deeply involved in the studies of electrolyte balance. A few bottles of urine were sitting on a cart and I guessed that the other bottles near the elevator would eventually end up here.

Figure 17. (a) The hardworking technicians. From left: Ruth Fleischmann, Marie Ellen Crofton and Betty Lawrence. (b) Betty Lawrence running the columns to measure levels of 17-hydroxycorticosteroids in blood.

Out of this room and at the entrance of the narrow corridor were two pieces of furniture that did not appear to belong to each other. It was explained that one was a muffle furnace that went to a very high temperature in order to activate various earths needed for column chromatography. The other was a refrigerator that belonged to Dr. Harold Harrison. On one side of this hot/cold system was the secretaries' office; Miss Mary Bachman and Mrs. Idaline

Ratcliffe were the ladies who had "worked untiringly on the preparation of the Zurich exhibit and on the manuscript" of the Wilkins book. When Miss Bachman retired, she was succeeded by Miss Eleanor Warfield, a distant cousin of Mrs. Warfield-Simpson who married the Duke of Windsor. Dr. Wilkins was very solicitous of his secretaries, often giving them a ride home. I must note that Baltimore is quite proud of its relationship with the British royalty as well as the Bonaparte family.

A door on the other side of the icebox entered into the Harrisons' laboratory. We went in and I met Dr. Helen Harrison who was a PhD doctor, working on calcium metabolism. I was told that her husband was the head of Pediatrics at Baltimore City Hospital; he was coming to the lab in the afternoon, the morning work being carried out by his wife.

Near the elevator was another large laboratory. This was the domain of Dr. Hugh Josephs who was a hematologist; he had been at Harriet Lane for many years. Dr. Josephs was a very soft-spoken and very kind gentleman. After his welcome words, we established that his wife, Dr. McCarthy, had been driving American ambulances in 1917-1918 in the northern part of the Allied front, near my hometown of Lens (Pas-de-Calais) in France. Dr. Wilkins was quite amazed; he explained that, at that time, he, too, was in France with the Hopkins group.

Leaving Dr. Josephs' lab, Dr. Wilkins passed the elevator and immediately we entered another lab that belonged to Endocrinology. On the left of that room, a low table was holding an instrument: a Geiger counter. Dr. Wilkins explained that the clinic used this counter to determine the radioactive iodine, ^{131}I, thyroid uptake of our patients, and that it was a very useful new methodology. Apparently, we shared the cost of the ^{131}I with Dr. Sam Asper in Adult Endocrinology. The radioactive iodine was sent directly to Hopkins from the Atomic Energy Commission. At the back of the room, in front of the windows, there was a high lab bench. Half of it was covered with papers belonging to Dr. John Crigler. Dr. Wilkins suggested that I could use the other half of the bench for reading and writing. Now I had an office!

Dr. Wilkins and I left this room but went no further: this was the limit of Pediatric Endocrinology. I was told that, at the other end of this building, were the laboratories of Dr. Victor Najjar and also a routine bacteriology lab for the pediatric patients, run by Mrs. Bonny Behner.

Dr. Wilkins concluded our tour, saying that this was all of the fifth floor of Harriet Lane. This floor had been added after the first four patient floors had been constructed. He also explained that it was rather hot here because of the structure of the building. Needless to say that, in those days, there was no air conditioning. I did not need Dr. Wilkins's explanation for understanding that this place was the closest to hell one could ever go unless one was actually in hell itself.

Indeed, this was an absolutely miserable environment in which everybody suffered but no one appeared to complain, so it was difficult for me to even comment. However, I must confess that I suffered a great deal for thirteen summers, until we moved to the new and air-conditioned Children's Medical and Surgical Center in 1963.

12

STUDENT LODGINGS AT HOPKINS

After this orientation, Dr. Wilkins sent me to find lodging. I first went to the Nurses Home on Broadway. The lady at the desk laughed at me: she explained that men were not permitted in the Nurses Home. I guess somebody felt that protection from males was needed for the nurses who at that time were all young ladies! I went back to the hospital where I had been told House Staff were lodged. Indeed I found a room but only for one week. After that I managed to find a room, again in the hospital but this time under the Dome. These were much larger rooms with windows looking right on Broadway. I was told that they were usually reserved for Chief Residents. I wonder whether present administrators who occupy these offices now know what went on in the early days in this space. After hours, the residents would meet, have great discussions and sing songs with one of them playing a guitar. Right under the Dome there was also a ping-pong table where many a disputed game was played. It was also a fact that it was not quite as sex-segregated as the Nurses' Home.

When I reported this observation to Dr. Wilkins, he stated that the House Staff members could do what they wanted when off duty. He added that, at the time of Prohibition when he was a medical student, ingenious colleagues had learned how to ferment various mixtures in the bathtubs of their rooms and to distill the brew into a strong but ugly alcohol. With time, the students had refined their technique: adding orange juice and sugar to the distillate that resulted in something resembling Grand Marnier. And we both laughed. What amazed me was I could comfortably discuss such escapades with my new Chief and I enjoyed it.

My room under the Dome was also a temporary lodging. Next, I moved to a fraternity house that was located on Broadway, across from the hospital.

This too was very temporary. These fraternity houses were replaced a few years later by a church and a Holiday Inn, which were replaced a few years later by the present Outpatient Building.

Eventually, I learned about another French fellow, Dr. Jacques Monier of Toulouse who was working with Drs. Eleanor Bliss and Caroline Chandler studying new antibiotics in the department of Dr. Perrin H. Long at the School of Hygiene. Dr. Wilkins explained to me that Dr. Long was a pioneer in the study of chemotherapy starting with sulfonamides.

I told him that I had been impressed with this therapy: the American soldiers in France seemed to all have a plastic box with sulfa powder that they used on any of their wounds with great results.

Jacques Monier had come with his wife, Evelyn, a nurse who was working at the Hopkins Nursing School. The three of us decided to rent a small row house on Madeira Street, near the Monument Street Food Market. I had discussed that option with Dr. Wilkins who thought that it was a good option; it would give me some relief from the English language! He laughed when I told him that every evening, Evelyn and Jacques prepared a large glass of water with a bunch of aspirin tablets, each of us being given a part of the glass in proportion to the hardship of our day.

For distraction, we bought a second-hand record player, but very few discs. I told Dr. Wilkins that now I knew by heart the violin concerto of Beethoven as played by the Philadelphia Orchestra directed by Eugene Ormandy with Zino Francescatti playing the violin. Dr. Wilkins confessed that he had received violin lessons in his youth but that he was not very fond of high-brow music; he preferred Gilbert and Sullivan's music and he proceeded to give me a few bars from the *Pirates of Penzance*. He always had a way to be warm and gracious.

After one year, the Moniers went back to Toulouse, but I stayed on. Dr. Wilkins had obtained support for me from the André and Bella Meyer Foundation for a second year of fellowship. I moved to a third-floor apartment above the Fish Laundry at the corner of Broadway and Monument Street, very close to Hopkins but with lots of rats in the backyard at night. I shared this apartment with Gordon Kennedy, a physician from Cambridge, England, who had come to work in our Pediatric Endocrine Clinic. I don't know where

Lawson and Gordon had met. Gordon was an expert studying brain lesions in rats, which resulted in polyphagia and obesity. Wilkins was impressed by it, and interested in that work.

Gordon was an outspoken man who expressed himself in a forward fashion. One day, Gordon and I met Wilkins, who appeared overjoyed in announcing that Mr. Winston Churchill had been elected. Gordon, a very liberal person, answered: "That big sh—." Personally, I was upset by his remark and I left the room, trying to avoid further conversation about it. This difference of opinion did not affect our friendship. A few years later the Wilkins went to visit the Kennedys in Cambridge and later, I went to see Gordon and his wife in their home, a fun experience with a lot of pints at the pubs! As to Mr. Churchill, his premiership was quite short and he retired from the political arena.

13

IN MY NEW OFFICE WITH
DR. JOHN CRIGLER

Sharing an office with Dr. John Crigler was an important way to get information on the Pediatric Endocrine Clinic and its chief, Dr. Lawson Wilkins.

John was very loquacious. So first, I learned that he had entered Johns Hopkins Medical School in 1939, the year he got married to his lovely wife, Marie Adele, who had a marvelous Southern accent from North Carolina. He had started an internship in Medicine but shortly thereafter he joined the US Navy in World War II. This statement raised my interest as I had been involved in WWII. On D-Day, he was on one of the boats (probably in the second wave) as a physician. He stayed on his boat, under plane attacks, tending to wounded men.

Figure 18. John Crigler, one of the early fellows. (April 2000)

I explained that, during the war, I volunteered in a small hospital in Rethel (Ardennes). The physician in charge decided to put the patients in the basement to avoid the bombs. I helped to transport them to the cave by passing through a huge open courtyard. When we were halfway there, we encountered machine gun fire from a plane passing over us but they missed. At that point, we ran for shelter.

John and I both enjoyed sharing our adventures, including the hits and misses. And we certainly talked about much more.

The following is what John Crigler wrote as a historical summary of the highlights of the Wilkins era at Johns Hopkins:

Years 1935-1946

Wilkins organized the first subspecialty Clinic of Pediatric Endocrinology in the world. He initiated longitudinal clinical observations, especially of physical growth and development of infants, children and adolescents with growth disorders and endocrinopathies. He also established a biological laboratory under the direction of Dr. Walter Fleischmann, a refugee from Nazi Germany who was a distinguished biochemist. He carried out hormonal and metabolic studies in animals and human beings.

His principal research interests were the following: thyroid disorders and the effect of thyroid hormone on skeletal growth and epiphyseal development and on creatine/creatinine and cholesterol metabolism; beginning of studies on abnormalities and variations of sexual development during childhood and adolescence including the publication with Drs. Fleischmann and John Eager Howard of papers describing "Macrogenitosomia precox associated with hyperplasia of the androgenic tissue of the adrenal and death from corticoadrenal insufficiency" in 1940, "The metabolic and growth effects of various androgens in sexually immature dwarfs" in 1942, and, without Howard, "Ovarian agenesis: pathology, associated clinical symptoms and the bearing on the theories of sex differentiation" in 1944 and "The influence of various androgenic steroids on nitrogen balance and growth" in 1946.

It is important to note that all of this was accomplished while Dr. Wilkins carried on a large full-time practice and without compensation from Hopkins. Evident during this time was his broad interest and involvement in clinical endocrinology (minus diabetes mellitus) as he established the program with an investigative focus on the metabolic effects of thyroid and steroid hormones. Dr. Wilkins's ability to work with associates in other departments such as Dr. Howard in Medicine and Dr. Young in Urology significantly enhanced the development of his program. It also was during this time that he attended a periodic (I believe it was at least yearly) get-together of a very select group of endocrinologists (from basic science—Dobriner, Pincus, etc. and internists—Albright, etc.) who essentially became his mentors and he their mentor in human developmental endocrinology. I suspect the group had a name but I don't remember it at this time if it ever had one. Dr. Albright was the individual in this group who had the biggest impact on Dr. Wilkins.

Years 1946-1950

Wilkins became full time at Hopkins; he established a postgraduate training program as we recognize it today. He published the first textbook of *Pediatric Endocrinology* (1950), importantly based on his meticulously documented and systematically organized and recorded longitudinal clinical observations related to pathophysiologic mechanisms. He reported the unsuccessful treatment of an infant with salt-losing congenital adrenocortical hyperplasia (CAH) with total adrenalectomy(5) and the successful suppression of androgen began our first experience with using cortisone in such patients. For me, it was a Baltimore summer spent maintaining the well-being of salt-losers under study and working with a flame photometer in a closed room (without air conditioning), which was the beginning of the long-term studies on salt-losing CAH carried out during my year as a fellow and subsequently reported.(6) What remarkable luck to come along at such a time and to be with such great colleagues.

We had weekly conferences with the endocrine group from the Department of Medicine under Dr. Howard, weekly Saturday clinics, and continuing studies on the effect of various glucocorticoids on the hormonal and metabolic responses of patients with different manifestations of CAH that resulted in a series of papers in *Journal of Clinical Endocrinology and Metabolism* in 1951-1952 and defined some of the pharmacological requirements for longer term treatment via different compounds and routes, dose and schedule of administration.

14

ESTABLISHING THE TREATMENT OF CONGENITAL ADRENAL HYPERPLASIA (CAH)

For the readers who are not endocrinologists, it might be helpful to outline our present knowledge of CAH. It is an inborn error of metabolism caused by a mutation of one of the genes that encodes the enzymes needed for cortisol and aldosterone synthesis from cholesterol. As it is an autosomal recessive disorder, both parents must contribute a mutant gene to the affected child. More than 90 percent of CAH cases are due to a deficiency of 21-hydroxylase, an enzyme the gene for which is located on chromosome 6, in the middle of the very important HLA genes: HLA A, B, C, DR, DP and DQ.

In major 21-hydroxylase deficiency, both cortisol and aldosterone secretion are deficient, resulting in the *salt-losing form of CAH*. In milder deficiency, only cortisol synthesis is affected: the *simple virilizing form* of the syndrome. In both forms, the output of adrenal androgens is excessive because of oversecretion of ACTH and accumulation of precursors of cortisol, which generate androgen synthesis. This will cause masculinization of the external genitalia of female fetuses including enlarged clitoris and variable degrees of fusion of the labia.

This knowledge was not available in 1950 when I arrived at Harriet Lane. John Crigler gave me a succinct review of what was already known about CAH and its treatment.

Three or four years earlier, Lawson Wilkins and Walter Fleischman along with Roger Lewis and Robert Klein had attempted to treat these patients with various synthetic steroids in the hope of suppressing the excessive production of androgens by their adrenal glands. Although these studies had generated interesting data on the anabolic effects of those various steroids, they failed to suppress the production of androgens in CAH. Fuller Albright at the Mass General Hospital in Boston had proposed that the adrenal cortex of human subjects was secreting three major groups of hormones; one he called the "sugar hormone," another was the "salt-retaining hormone" the third was the "adrenal androgens." On the basis of this model it was easy to visualize that the abnormality in CAH was overproduction of the male hormone with a decreased secretion of the sugar and salt-retaining hormones. Roger Lewis, Robert Klein and Lawson Wilkins had shown that the administration of ACTH to CAH patients produced a further increase in adrenal androgens measured as urinary 17-ketosteroids. At the same time they observed that ACTH administration caused a greater disturbance in the salt balance suggesting that perhaps ACTH was increasing the secretion of a salt-losing hormone.

With a great deal of pride, John Crigler explained to me that many major endocrinologists at Hopkins had been involved in the preparation of adrenal extracts, which could help the salt-loss of patients with Addison disease. And he cited the names of George Harrop, George Thorn, Harry Eisenberg, Lewis Engel and John Eager Howard. In the late 1930s, Reichstein and colleagues in Basel synthesized deoxycorticosterone acetate (DOCA). This steroid did help the salt imbalance but did not correct the hypoglycemia.

Dr. Wilkins added to this conversation, stating that the sugar hormone, 11-dehydro-17-hydroxy-corticosterone, now known as cortisone, had been isolated from extracts of the adrenal cortex by Dr. Kendall at the Mayo Clinic in the mid-1940s. A sample of this preparation had been given to Dr. George Thorn who showed that it was effective in correcting the hypoglycemia of patients with Addison disease (adrenal insufficiency). It took several more years for the Merck Company to synthesize cortisone acetate in amounts large enough for therapeutic trials.

In early 1949, cortisone acetate was used to treat patients with chronic arthritis. I remember a movie that showed patients unable to ambulate before treatment. After two weeks of cortisone acetate, they were able to walk and step up on a ladder. This was the first use of the new hormone.

In late 1949, Dr. Wilkins, along with Drs. Roger Lewis, Robert Klein and Eugenia Rosenberg, studied a fifteen-year-old girl with CAH. When she was six years old, part of her adrenal glands had been removed by Dr. Hugh H. Young but this did not influence the excessive adrenal androgen secretion. However, the administration of 100 mg of cortisone acetate daily for fifteen days dramatically suppressed her urinary excretion of androgens (17-ketosteroids). Simultaneously, Fred Bartter and the endocrine group at the Massachusetts General Hospital in Boston obtained similar results. This was a great achievement in the treatment of abnormal adrenal function. The first patient with salt-loss who survived is shown on her first birthday in Figure 19.

Further investigation by Wilkins and his fellows, as well as other researchers illuminated the pathophysiology of CAH.

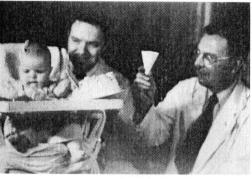

Figure 19. Lois on her first birthday with Lytt Gardner and Lawson Wilkins. Lois was the first baby with the salt-losing form of congenital adrenal hyperplasia who survived with treatment of cortisone, salt retaining hormone. (1951)

We learned that the adrenal glands of these patients are unable to produce the "sugar hormone" (glucocorticoid, cortisol). In an effort to compensate for this, the pituitary gland secretes large amounts of ACTH resulting in excessive production of adrenal androgens. Treatment with cortisone replaces the missing sugar hormone and at the same time suppresses ACTH and androgen secretion.

From 1952 to 1955, Alfred Bongiovanni and Walter Eberlein were at Hopkins, studying the steroid metabolism in CAH patients. They concluded that there was a block in the steroid biosynthesis at the level of the 21-hydroxylase. It resulted in insufficient secretion of cortisol with an increase in precursors such as 17-hydroxy-progesterone, which were metabolized to the virilizing androgens.

15

LEARNING HOW TO MEASURE THE URINARY EXCRETION OF STEROID METABOLISM

After my short indoctrination on the treatment of CAH, I asked Dr. Wilkins how I could help. At that time, we knew that cortisone acetate treatment could suppress the adrenal androgens. However, very quickly it became evident that it was important to determine the minimal amount of cortisone needed to suppress the adrenal cortex as excessive amounts resulted in signs of Cushing syndrome. The only means available to determine the degree of androgen suppression was the measurement of the twenty-four-hour urinary excretion of 17-ketosteroids (17-KS). Hence, patients were admitted to the hospital, and given various amounts of cortisone. Urine collection was a key step in the study and the measurement of 17-KS was a tangible endpoint.

There were many problems in measuring the urinary excretion of 17-KS. It was most important that the twenty-four-hour urine collection be complete. This was difficult enough in toilet-trained children, but it was a major problem in infants. The Harriet Lane nurses devised ingenious means for urine collections in both boys and girls. Another problem was the storage of the urine samples. The small cold-room was overflowing with urine bottles. Freezers had to be purchased as it seemed important to store some samples for further investigations at a later date.

The laboratory technicians, Mary Ellen Crafton and Henry Schulte, and shortly thereafter Betty Youngblood-Lawrence, were expected to run all the tests. However, the volume of work was overwhelming. So, I was most welcome to learn how to measure the "ketos"—boiling an aliquot of acidified urine, extracting steroids with ether using separatory funnels, washing the extract with sodium hydroxide and water, carefully evaporating the ether and then, carrying out a Zimmermann color reaction on the extract. All together, we did thousands of Zimmermann reactions and "ketos" measurements.

One day, out of nowhere, appeared a middle-aged gentleman who introduced himself. "I am Dr. Zimmermann, with two *"Ns"* at the end, of the Zimmermann reaction." I was quite surprised as I expected the man to be part of past history. When I presented Dr. Zimmermann to Lawson, I believe that he was also surprised but he did not forget to ask him to sign his visitors' book. Later, I realized that, in our publications, we had used only one "N" at the end of his name!

The laboratory performed several tests in addition to the 17-KS assay. There was the bioassay for gonadotropins using immature mice. We measured urinary 11-oxosteroids and total estrogens. This latter was measured as "estroids" in urine.

Because urinary "estroids" were elevated in untreated CAH and decreased with cortisone treatment, I suggested to Dr. Wilkins that further studies were needed. He agreed that it was an important question. In order to carry out estrogen bioassays, he helped me contact Dr. W.W. Scott in Urology. Then, he arranged for me to visit Dr. Lewis Engle's lab in Boston and paid my travel expenses. This is how I got involved in the separation of the various estrogens—estrone, estradiol, and estriol by counter-current distribution. When I wrote the results for publication, I asked Dr. Wilkins to review and correct my text. The next day, he returned my paper with no corrections, along with a new edition of this paper, fully hand-written by him. He explained that it was easier for him to rewrite rather than correct. I had the hand-written version typed by the secretary and made sure that Lawson Wilkins was an author. I resubmitted the paper to him and it came back to me with two corrections: Lawson's name was deleted from the front page and an acknowledgment to Dr. Wilkins was added at the end.

On that day, I realized that under the cover of roughness suggested by the gruff voice, there was a huge amount of generosity and warmth in this man. On that day he became more than my mentor; he was more like a father.

16

ESTABLISHING THE DETAILS OF TREATMENT OF PATIENTS WITH CAH

In the evening of each working day, the ketos results were posted on each patient file. The files were pinned on bulletin boards in the secretaries' office. After the secretaries had left, Dr. Wilkins was joined by Lytt Gardner, John Crigler and me. Often, there would be one or two interns as well as one of the numerous visitors. Long discussions would take place about modifying the treatment of each patient. Some studies compared results obtained with oral versus intramuscular cortisone or compared cortisone to cortisol or to corticosterone. These sessions were fascinating. Anyone could give an opinion but the discussion was usually dominated by the deep bass voice of Dr. Wilkins and the high-pitched voice of John Crigler.

In the early '50s, it seemed that everybody smoked. Our little meeting room would rapidly fill with the smoke of burning cigarettes. Dr. Wilkins was the worst; each day he would come with two packs but often it was not enough; we knew to have cigarettes available for him at the end of the day in order to fill the gap. We joked that Dr. Wilkins used only one match per day, the one that lit his first cigarette.

It seems that out of these daily meetings came the elaboration of the proper treatment for CAH patients. We learned that oral cortisone acetate had to be given three times a day, whereas IM cortisone acetate could be given once every three days. Further, the IM preparation was twice as potent as the oral tablets. An additional observation was that some patients presented in acute adrenal crisis with salt-loss in the first five to seven days of life (salt-losing form) whereas others presented with masculinization and hirsutism only (simple virilizing form). (Figure 20)

Figure 20. Claude Migeon with one of the very first nonsalt-losing patients. (1990)

17

THE PSYCHOHORMONAL
RESEARCH UNIT

Shortly after my arrival at Hopkins, Dr. Wilkins mentioned to me that he had met in Boston a young man from New Zealand who was finishing his PhD at Harvard. The subject of his thesis was the study of patients with abnormalities of sex differentiation including patients with congenital adrenal hyperplasia. His name was John W. Money. Wilkins thought that this man would be of great help with the many patients we were seeing in our clinic who had various problems of sex differentiation.

I cannot do better than to quote Dr. Wilkins in the preface of the Second Edition of his textbook:

> We have been most fortunate to have working with our group of pediatric endocrinologists a team in Psychology and Psychiatry, John W. Money, PhD, Joan L. Hampson, MD and John G. Hampson, MD, under a special grant from the Josiah Macy, Jr. Foundation. Their studies and management of the psychological problems of adjustment, which confront the patients with various types of endocrine disorders have been of the greatest benefit to us and to the patients. In addition, the endocrinopathies produced deviation from the normal path of somatic and sexual development, which presents an extraordinary opportunity to evaluate the relative roles of environmental, hormonal, and chromosomal factors in determining psychology patterns. Some of their findings have had a profound influence on fundamental concepts of psychosexual development.

Indeed John Money and Joan and John Hampson were extremely helpful in the management of our pediatric endocrine patients. John Money described it well in the preface of the Third Edition of the Lawson Wilkins textbook:

There was another sequel of the adrenogenital story for which Wilkins has not, until now, received the proper amount of recognition; namely the establishment of a new psychohormonal research unit for the study of psychology of hermaphroditism and related endocrine disorders. This psychological research has increased fundamental knowledge of the process of psychosexual differentiation relative to genetic and hormonal variables and the sex of rearing. It is a sign of Wilkins's breadth of intellect that he surmounted a traditional bond of prejudice and sponsored psychological investigation in his clinic...

The work of the Psychohormonal Research Unit raised a great deal of controversy. It was suggested that Money was ignoring "nature" and overemphasizing "nurture" in the nature/nurture conflict in matters of psychosexuality. In fact, the Research Unit has all along recognized the dual effects of both nature and nurture.

18

DR. WILKINS'S SATURDAY MORNING CLINIC

Dr. Wilkins saw patients almost every morning. This included Saturday. He would see a limited number of patients—three or four—at each clinic. Each day one of the fellows would help him with the clinic in "Observation 3" (down in the lower floor of the Harriet Lane Home).

Every clinic of the week was interesting and educational. However, the Saturday Morning Clinic was the jewel of them all. Dr. Wilkins would specifically schedule patients with unusual conditions or with a long follow-up that would permit a critical evaluation of the therapeutic results.

The entire staff of the Pediatric Endocrine Clinic was expected to attend. On occasion, I would attempt to finish an experiment in my lab. Chances of escaping from Saturday Clinic were nil; Dr. Wilkins would make a run to the fifth Floor, asking Odessa to hold the elevator for his return downstairs. Quickly, he would come to tell me that there were very important cases to be discussed. And, of course, I would rush down with him to the conference room.

The large conference room with two sofas in a circle was available for discussion. Each patient would first be seen by one of us in an observation room, and then the history would be presented with great detail in the conference room. Dr. Wilkins would ask advice of the attendees who might have special knowledge of the problem and discussion would ensue, new ideas would be debated.

In addition to our Staff, there were usually two or three interns and residents. There would also be visitors from the United States or abroad. Dr. Marvin Cornblath, a pediatrician serving in the Army at Fort Dietrich in Frederick, Maryland would attend every week. John Money and his assistants of the Psychohormonal group were part of the group. Dr. Wilkins would also invite members of Pathology or the Medicine faculty to discuss unusual disorders.

Every clinic was a great success and by 1:30 p.m. we would all rush to the "Doctors Dining Room," which closed at 2:00 p.m. We would sit at a large round table where the discussion of the cases would continue. Every time Dr. Wilkins would conclude, "That was a good clinic," partially as self-satisfaction but also justified by the interesting comments of the various experts.

Sometimes, Dr. Helen Taussig would join us for lunch. She was very pleasant. It was said that when she did not like the discussions, she would turn off her hearing aid system.

19

EXPERIMENTAL WORK AND
LANGUAGE DIFFICULTIES

The Pediatric Endocrine Clinic under Dr. Wilkins provided a stimulating environment and an atmosphere of enthusiasm for research. At our Journal Club, we all contributed to the discussion of recent publications. One novel idea, brought to my attention, was the effect of DDT (dichlorodiphenyltrichloroethane) on humans and particularly on the adrenal gland. Dr. Wilkins and Dr. Gardner suggested to me that experimental work on dogs and might be useful in clearing up this problem.

Arrangements were made through Dr. Stanley Eversol, the Chief Resident in Pathology to provide six dogs who would be caged on the top floor of the Pathology Building. After much discussion with Dr. Wilkins, we agreed on a specific protocol. Every day I would go and visit the dogs, to check on the amount of DDT that was fed to them with their regular diet. I was told that the dogs were well taken care of and exercised every day. We carried out the Thorn test of adrenal function, which involved an eosinophil count before and four hours after an injection of ACTH, twice a week.

Then one day I found that two of the experimental dogs had baby dogs in their cages. I was also told the third one, a female, was also pregnant.

It became clear that the exercise that the dogs were taking was communal. It was also clear that treatment with DDT did not decrease the interest of the male dogs for their female partners. That day when I came back from the Pathology building to Harriet Lane, I was very distraught. When Dr. Wilkins asked me how the experiment was going, I told him that the dogs had "poopies." Lytt Gardner, who was close to us, added, "Claude means puppies." Well, Dr. Wilkins had a good laugh, and at that point I realized that not only my experimental work was a fiasco but that also I had created folklore for the future. In fact when my name came up in a conversation, Dr. Wilkins would say, "Claude doesn't work anymore with dogs because they have poopies."

Dr. Wilkins loved to have fun and in the process, I learned how to pronounce certain words properly.

On another occasion when I had visited Boston I had stayed overnight with friends of Lytt Gardner. On my return, I had asked Dr. Wilkins how I should express my thanks. He suggested I could send a little note to the hostess. I did so and later presented my draft to him. At that point he said, "Claude, I think you might want to change the sentence, which goes, 'Thank you very much; I very much enjoyed the night I spent with you.' I would replace the word 'night' with 'evening.'" I realized what I had written and we both smiled. The fifth floor of Harriet Lane, specifically the Pediatric Endocrine group, was the site of a lot of hard work, a lot of scientific discussions, and also a lot of fun.

20

RIDING WITH DR. WILKINS

On a first encounter with Lawson Wilkins, most would have considered him quite somber. Most of the time, he would appear very serious. He usually wore a charcoal suit with a white or blue shirt with a button-down collar and a dark tie. Once, he took me to S. Schwartz, a large discount retailer, as we both needed a new suit. I settled on a light brown. Dr. Wilkins bought another charcoal suit.

This sullen appearance was a cover-up for a very sociable and congenial personality. Dr. Wilkins loved to talk. Indeed he had a deep need to communicate, to share his own thoughts.

Often he was invited to give lectures at the NIH and the Naval Hospital in Bethesda and at the Union Memorial Hospital in Baltimore. Sometimes he would give a series of lectures covering the major aspects of Pediatric Endocrinology. Almost routinely, he would ask if I wanted to come along, suggesting that I might be interested in the subject of the lectures or that I might help in showing the slides. Each time, it was an occasion for a trip in his car. And of course, it was an opportunity for conversation. In my early days in Baltimore, my English was poorly enunciated and not easy to understand.

So, Dr. Wilkins would carry out the major part of the discussion. We considered many subjects, ranging from aspects of the work in the clinic, to the personality of people at Hopkins and outside of Hopkins.

One day, driving on Broadway from Fells Point to Hopkins Hospital, we stopped in front of 6 North Broadway. There was an elegant brick house with a stone base where his father practiced medicine and where Lawson was raised as a child. The side of the house was on a small alley. Dr. Wilkins showed me the garage where the horse and buggy had been kept. He had great memories of the horse and buggy used by his dad to visit his patients. He remembered the first motorcars, which had trouble going up the hill of South Broadway. Sometimes, with other kids, he would give the weak cars a helpful push up the hill. And he remembered what great fun it was.

This was also the house where, at the time of the great Baltimore fire, he was kept on his knees with his sister in order to pray for the safety of the city when he would rather have watched this great fire, and the firemen fighting it.

21

SKIP'S ACCIDENT (JANUARY 15, 1944)

Another time, driving on Cold Spring and arriving at Dolfield Avenue, Dr. Wilkins told me that this was where his sixteen-year-old son had been killed. In the winter of 1943-1944, Skip had a Christmas job driving a post office truck. Another car ran into him and he was ejected out of his seat. Dr. Wilkins would further describe how he had to identify his dead son at the morgue. One could almost palpate the depth of his sorrow. Saying that I was sorry did not come close to match the sadness of Lawson. And a silence would take over for a while.

The subject of his son would come up quite often, usually in late evening, after he had a few glasses of rye whiskey. "I guess Skip was not a scholar, but he was a kind boy" or "I don't think Skip would have made it in medical school." Then the tone of his voice would go deeper and its volume would go down, before a short silence. Then, the conversation would resume on another subject. (Figure 8)

There was an incredible mournful sadness in Dr. Wilkins's soul when it came to the loss of his son. But I would give a totally wrong impression if I had suggested that he was a sad person. On occasion, after a hot day on the fifth floor of Harriet Lane, he would bring me to his house on Edgevale Road. In summer, when we would hit University Parkway, he would note that the temperature had gone down at least five degrees and that was good! And since it was still daylight, we could have a game of croquet in the backyard with Mrs. Wilkins. These sessions were riotously funny.

22

A CHRISTMAS DINNER IN BALTIMORE (DECEMBER 1950)

Both Dr. Wilkins and Lucile had a great interest in French cooking. They asked me to describe a typical French Christmas dinner. I explained that, in my family, this was a very elaborate meal, lasting from noon to late in the evening, usually including soup, fish, turkey, vegetables, dessert with wines, champagne and coffee. Dr. Wilkins became excited and wanted to experience such a dinner. He proposed that Lucile, Mary Adele Crigler and Lockley Gardner could fetch all the ingredients needed. All I would have to do is make the appropriate list of supplies and organize the ladies, who would do the work in the kitchen and the dining room. How I let them convince me that it would be easy I shall never know. The site for the now famous dinner was the row house on Wolfe Street where the Criglers lived. The date was chosen as a Sunday night before Christmas, as everyone had previous commitments for December 25.

Several weeks ahead of the date, I communicated with my aunt who sent me a recipe for the "Buche de Noël," the traditional Christmas cake, shaped like a log, which was very difficult to make! Every day, Dr. Wilkins wanted reassurance that I had not forgotten anything on my list, requesting supplies, particularly the wines. Mrs. Wilkins, Mrs. Gardner and Mrs. Crigler were busy finding the essential ingredients. Buying a turkey was easy, but finding the truffles to slip under the skin was much more difficult. Dr. Wilkins told me that the ladies had to take a trip to Washington, DC, to purchase a little can of truffles, and that it was amazingly expensive!

As the day of the festivity came closer, the excitement grew. On several days, I went to rehearse my helpers. Who was going to prepare the homemade mayonnaise ahead of time? This required Dijon mustard (real!), peanut oil and very fresh eggs. When would the green beans and potatoes be prepared? Dr. Wilkins found out that "colin," the fish that I needed, was "hake" in English. From his home, he brought the proper container for poaching the fish, and a long plate to lay the "colin" for serving. Mrs. Wilkins obtained the chestnuts for the stuffing of the turkey. Mrs. Gardner purchased the French unsalted butter and the pistachio for the Buche de Noel.

Early Sunday morning, I came to the Crigler's home. I started with the "Buche de Noel", cooking the sponge cake and preparing the chocolate-butter cream. This could be done in advance and kept in the icebox. The same for the "colin." I had a problem with it: when I tried to remove the skin and bones, it all fell apart. But, with my hands I rebuilt a fish shape on a bed of leaves of lettuce on the serving plate, and then covered the irregularities with mayonnaise that I made myself. For the turkey, I made small cuts in the skin and introduced a thin slice of truffle between skin and meat. My lady-helpers took care of the chestnuts: we added a very small amount of bread stuffing and, most importantly, a small glass of cognac. The helpers also took charge of the cooking. Then, for the soup, I used beef bouillon, adding onions sautéed in butter. Before serving it, we added bread croutons and grated Swiss cheese. Preparing the green beans and potatoes was fairly simple. They were spiced with garlic, parsley, and lots of butter.

A great discussion had taken place the previous day about an apértif before the meal. Lytt Gardner, a well-recognized expert in mint juleps had offered his services. Lawson preferred Scotch. I had proposed the French sweet vermouth, Cinzano. Eventually, we agreed that as they would spoil the meal, pre-dinner drinks could be dispensed with. So, here is the memorable menu:

Christmas 1950

Pediatric Endocrine Clinic
Harriet Lane Home
Baltimore

Soupe á l'onion

Colin au Persil
Chablis

Dinde Truffée
Chataignes—Haricot Verts—Pommes Sautées
Chateau Neuf du Pape

Buche de Nöel
Champagne Vve Cliquot

Café—*Grand Marnier*

This was quite a feast! The Grand Marnier liqueur brought up the story of Lawson making some orange liqueur when he and his colleagues were medical students. This was done with oranges, their peels and of course, alcohol. The maceration took place in the interns' bathtubs at Hopkins, hidden from the authorities. This, in turn brought up the story of the Hopkins Unit in France during WWI. An officer called Lawson and his colleague student-soldiers to attention. Their names were read and it was announced that they had received their MD degree. This was their graduation ceremony. After that, they were told to go back to their occupation: on that day, it was latrine duty!

Needless to say that in the following days, Lawson Wilkins reported to whoever was willing to listen the story of this memorable dinner. He would describe with great detail how I handled each individual crouton, in order to make sure that they were all grilled just right on every side. He also told how he had to carve a turkey, which had truffle bruises all over its skin! "But it was magnifique!"

23

CELEBRATING THE NEW YEAR IN CHICAGO WITH FRIENDS (JANUARY 1951)

Dr. Wilkins had invited me to join his family for the New Year. He said that I was not asked to help with the cooking, like I did for Christmas. He noted that the dinner might not be as good but it would be great fun.

I had to explain that I was going to Chicago to visit my friends, Bill and Stella Nanos. I explained that I had met them in Paris, that we had created a great amity and love. Together, we had visited the grave of their brother who had died while he was with the American troops at Bastogne, Belgium on Christmas Day of 1944. Of course, he understood and made me promise that I would visit him when I got back.

Indeed, I did tell Lawson about my Chicago trip. Not all at once, but on several occasions while we were driving together. One time, I explained that my friends, the Nanos, were of Greek origin. Stella had a Master's degree in Biology and she trained with Dr. Papanicolaou, the man who established the "Pap smear." Stella directed the cytology lab at the hospital of the University of Illinois. Bill was involved with buying books for the students at the University of Illinois.

It was so nice to be together again and my friends had a marvelous surprise for me: they had tickets for the show *South Pacific* with the original cast: Mary Martin and Ezio Pinza. The musical is based on the book *Tales of the South Pacific* by James Michener. The 1949 Broadway production had music by Richard Rodgers and text by Oscar Hammerstein.

One of the songs, sung by a little girl, is in French:

- Dites moi pourquoi la vie est belle

- Dites moi pourquoi la vie est gai

- Est-ce que c'est parce que vous m'aimez?

III

Martin was wonderful when she sang "I'm Gonna Wash That Man Right Outta My Hair" while Pinza was marvelous singing "Some Enchanted Evening." I told Wilkins that the show was terrific and that he should see it, which he did later in New York City. He loved it as much as I did.

The week with my friends was quite short. With some of their friends, we went to the best French restaurant in Chicago, visited the art museum, whose numerous paintings by French Impressionists amazed me.

I do have to say that the weather was quite rough with snow and wind coming from Lake Michigan. I had no problem with my flight back to Baltimore, except for the sadness to say goodbye to Bill and Stella Nanos.

24

PRESENTATION OF THE RESULTS OF THE TREATMENT OF CONGENITAL ADRENAL HYPERPLASIA WITH SALT-LOSS: ATLANTIC CITY (JUNE 1951)

In 1950 and 1951, all of us, especially John Crigler, had focused our attention on the treatment of infants with the salt-losing form of congenital adrenal hyperplasia. First, we found that these infants needed cortisone as well as the salt-retaining hormone. At that time, the only preparation available was 11-deoxycorticosterone acetate (DOCA); it could be given IM daily or as a DOCA pellet implanted under the skin of the shoulder and it would last about twelve to eighteen months. The great lesson from our study was that salt-losing patients were quite labile and very difficult to control. Indeed, they seemed to require almost daily observation with frequent adjustments to their treatment in order to maintain their salt and water balance.

At that time we found that the implantation of a DOCA pellet along with the IM cortisone acetate given every third day was the optimal treatment of these patients. Unfortunately, today the DOCA pellets and the IM cortisone acetate are no longer available (not profitable enough). Because of this, one must use *oral* preparations of cortisol or prednisolone, and fludrocortisone. This indeed makes it much more difficult to maintain electrolyte balance in those salt-losing infants.

You need to know that before the availability of cortisol and DOCA the patients with the salt-losing form of CAH would die in infancy or early childhood. We investigated the age of death: mainly they died at a few weeks of age, a few survived a few months. It was therefore quite exciting for all of us to put our data together and prepare our presentation of the promising results at the meeting of the Endocrine Society in Atlantic City.

A trip to Atlantic City in 1951 was an adventure. Dr. Wilkins decided that John Crigler and I would drive with him. At that time, there was no Delaware Memorial Bridge and the only way to cross the Delaware River was by ferryboat. This was not a very long voyage, but putting the car on the boat and crossing the river was quite enough excitement. This was indeed an occasion to take pictures as a memory of the voyage.

Dr. Wilkins had arranged the hotel reservation; an extra bed was added to a room with twin beds so the three of us could share a very large room. During the trip, as well as in the room, Dr. Wilkins would discuss with us many of the patients whose studies would be presented at the meeting by John Crigler. The talk was extremely well-received, and the question period ran well over the allotted time. After the session, all three of us were questioned by many physicians who wanted more information and details. Of course the big wheels talked mainly to Lawson, the younger fellows talked to John and me.

Figure 21. Lawson Wilkins and Claude Migeon on the ferry crossing the Susquehanna River on their way to an Atlantic City meeting. (June 1951)

Needless to say, this was all very exciting. One of the physicians who asked me a question was Dr. Maria New, starting a lifelong friendship. There were also several dinners with plenty of drinks. The time for bed was usually late in the night. Then at 6:30 a.m. we were awakened by Dr. Wilkins who had already taken his shower and was getting dressed, as he had a meeting at 7:00 a.m. for some committee of the Society. He seemed as fresh as a new rose. It was amazing for me to see how much energy this man had. As for me, I had a terrible hangover from too much alcohol and too much talking the night before.

25

VISIT TO HARVARD, MASSACHUSETTS, GENERAL HOSPITAL (JULY 1951)

Lytt Gardner, who had come to Hopkins from Boston in July of 1950, had many friends at "Mass General" where he had trained.

In July 1951, he planned to visit his old colleagues and asked me to go with him. I accepted and had a lot of fun. We stayed at Lytt's friend's home and visited the Department of Pediatrics at Mass General. I met some of the senior physicians, Nathan Talbot and Fred Bartter, as well as some junior investigators, Jack Crawford and Edna Sobel. Lytt had been part of the group. Robert Klein also happened to be visiting from Pittsburgh Children's Hospital. Bob had been a fellow of Wilkins from 1948-1950 with Roger Lewis (1946-1950) and Eugenia Rosemberg (1949-1950) who came from Buenos Aires. (Figure 22)

Figure 22. The fellows: From left: Claude Migeon, Lytt
Gardner and Robert Klein discussing data with Edna Sobel
at the Mass General Hospital in Boston. (1951)

Sitting down with coffee, I was told about Fuller Albright, the most distinguished clinical scientist. He had trained in calcium metabolism with Dr. Joseph Aub. Then he came to Hopkins to work with Dr. Warfield Longcope. During that time he worked in the lab with John Eager Howard. He also spent one year with the Viennese pathologist, Jakob Erdheim.

I did not see Dr. Albright during that visit. However, the following July of 1952, I was sitting near him at the Endocrine Society meeting. Despite the space between our seats, I could see the effects of Parkinson's disease on this giant of endocrine science. He was shaking a great deal and had abundant secretions running from his mouth and nose. His handkerchief was hanging from his pocket but he did not seem to be able to grab it. I sat there asking myself what one should do for such an important professor in that situation. I gathered my courage and reached into his pocket, grabbed his handkerchief, and placed it in his hand. He could not talk, but his eyes seemed to say thank you. I was glad that I could help him but felt so sad that he was in such need.

26

MAKING SOME BEAUTIFUL MUSIC

As I have previously noted, Dr. Wilkins was very gregarious and sociable. He would invite his fellows very often for an evening at his home. Some of these visits were to discuss science but others were just for fun. It seems that Lawson had no trouble finding an excuse for a party. (Figure 23)

Whatever the nature of the party, there was always a time for singing. Lucile Wilkins would play the piano and the rest of us would sing. Lawson loved all the old negro spirituals like "Go Down, Moses." He also liked French songs, his favorite one being:

Figure 23. The garden parties in Wilkins's backyard. Lawson talking with John Crigler and Janny van Walbeek of the Netherlands. (Summer 1951)

- Chevaliers de la table ronde
- Gôutons voir si le vin est bon,
- Gôutons voir, oui, oui, oui.
- Gôutons voir, non, non, non
- Gôutons voir si le vin est bon.

Lawson particularly appreciated the "wee, wee, wee." For this song, I was the leader of the singing group.

Anyone who has known Dr. Wilkins, must have heard him sing. Clearly, he was not great at keeping a tune, and his deep bass voice did not help the music. But, he loved to sing! So, we all sang and a little whiskey seemed to help keep the voices in tune.

At one time, Dr. Wilkins rediscovered his old violin. He told us that he had learned to play as a child and that he was practicing at night when he could not sleep. After a few months of practice, Lawson must have thought that he was ready for his entry on the music stage as he planned a soireé. He invited Dr. Harold Harrison who was a first class pianist and Dr. John Crigler who played the cello very well. There were also the regulars who made up the audience. After the three artistes had talked about the musical piece, they started playing. Quickly, something went wrong and Dr. Wilkins stopped playing. A second trial was made, just as disastrous as the first. And a third and a fourth attempt. At the fifth trial, Lawson was able to play for a short while but when the tempo accelerated, he was unable to keep up and he was begging, "Please, wait for me, wait for me!" Shortly thereafter the musical session ended. I have the feeling that it was also the end of violin playing for Lawson. But, it did not stop our singing that night, nor any night, with a glass of rye or bourbon in hand.

27

PREPARING TO RETURN TO PARIS (SUMMER 1952)

My travel expenses from France and my stay in Baltimore were covered by the Fulbright Foundation for twelve months at Johns Hopkins. After their year in the USA, the Fulbright Fellows were expected to return home.

Lawson Wilkins asked me about my plans and whether I would like to stay a second year. I was delighted. Then, Lawson made arrangements for me to receive support from the André and Bella Meyer Foundation and the American Friends Foundation. This was a wonderful opportunity for me as I expected the second year to be much more productive than the first one, which had included a lot of time to adapt to a new environment. And it was!

However, toward the end of my second year at Harriet Lane Home, I had to plan to return to Paris. Preliminary contacts in France suggested that my chances of continuing laboratory work and research that I had carried out at Hopkins were limited in Paris. Dr. Wilkins brought up the idea that I might consider returning to the United States and that, before I left for France, I might consider my possibilities in this country. He sent my CV and his personal recommendations to several of his endocrine friends around the country, and there were four encouraging responses. Dr. Wilkins suggested that I should go for interviews with Dr. Albert Segaloff at the Alton Ochsner Foundation in New Orleans and Dr. Jack Trunnell at M.D. Anderson Hospital in Houston. A letter of Dr. Leo T. (for Tolstoy) Samuels in Salt Lake City had an offer conditional on whether Don Nelson would leave for Boston.

There was also an offer of position by Dr. Sontag, Director of the Fels Research Institute for the Study of Human Development at Antioch College.

Finally, Dr. Seymour Lieberman at Columbia, whose laboratory I had visited on several occasions, also offered me a position, sending me a telegram: "Dr. Taylor (head of gynecology) offers you a Fellowship for one year beginning at your convenience."

This number of possibilities was amazing and scary at the same time. Dr. Wilkins fully shared this excitement. We would spend time in Baltimore analyzing each offer, the site and the people involved. The discussion continued by letter (at least one a week) while I was in France.

Just before leaving Baltimore, I had supper at the Wilkins' home and later in the evening, Lawson went through a full analysis of my long-range future. Lucile had left the two of us alone in the living room, Lawson standing up in front of the fireplace, his shoulders slightly vaulted, his left hand in his pocket, a cigarette in the right hand. I sat in an armchair, watching Lawson pace slowly back and forth. First, we discussed my chances to advance my career in Pediatric Endocrinology in Paris—a sub-specialty which did not exist in France at the time. Then he discussed the importance of biochemistry and physiology (at that time genetics did not dominate medical science) in biologic research. Lawson was so involved in this discussion that I had to rush with an ashtray in order to catch his long, drooping cigarette ashes. He made clear that Columbia and the University of Utah with their steroid training programs were the most advanced departments of Biochemistry in the area of steroid metabolism. Perhaps, Lawson's personal bias made him suggest that the extensive studies of Samuels on glucocorticoids were opening new horizons in adrenal research.

That evening was probably one of the most important steps in the direction of my future career in clinical research. We had a nightcap and I went home. In present parlance, Dr. Wilkins was my "mentor." I thought of him more as a very wise scientific father.

28

BACK TO PARIS
(OCTOBER-DECEMBER 1952)

The trip back to France on the "Liberté" was not very comfortable as the October Atlantic Ocean was not kind. Before my departure, the goodbyes were very warm but everyone seemed to be sure that I would be back shortly. And they were right.

I found my old "chambre de bonne" at 11 Bis Rue Cesar Franck. I went to visit the family at Rethel and Lens. The prospects in Paris were not great.

I kept a running correspondence with Dr. Wilkins. I explained the pleasure of seeing my family and friends but also the lack of positions in the French medical system, as expected. I went to Zurich, to visit Andrea Prader at the Kinderspital. I had met Andrea during his visit to Baltimore. European academic systems were quite rigid and there was no future for me in Switzerland. Meanwhile, Dr. Samuels had written to Lawson that Dr. Don Nelson had left for Boston and that he could offer me a position of Research Instructor. A specific requirement was that I should be in Salt Lake City by January 1953. Lawson let me know about it by telegram.

This was followed by a copy of Dr. Samuels's letter, which was forwarded by Lawson. On November 13, 1952, I sent a telegram and a letter of acceptance to Salt Lake City with copy to Dr. Wilkins.

On November 25, 1952, Lawson wrote:

"Dear Claude:

It was very nice to hear from you. I believe that you made the correct decision in accepting Samuels' offer, but I hope that I did not exert too much influence on you. I realize that it is a great disappointment not to go ahead with the problem of the unknown fluorogens, but I believe that what you will learn from Samuels about corticoids and other steroids will be most profitable and that you will find him very stimulating.

I hope that you do not have any trouble about the visa. Please let me know as soon as possible your plans for returning and be sure to stop in Baltimore. It was probably difficult for you to explain your decision to your family and friends. I trust they were able to understand and accept this as the best thing for you.

Al Bongiovanni is working most enthusiastically not only on the column chromatographic pattern of the urinary steroids but also on the pregnane compounds and the blood corticosteroids. He is studying the effects of ACTH on these in adrenal hyperplasias, normals and Cushings. We hope to learn whether there is an abnormality in the synthesis of the adrenal steroids. George Clayton is measuring the conversion rate of total plasma I^{131} to PBI^{131}. José and Walter are working on serum mucoproteins and urinary amino acid paper chromatography.

The only thing new to tell you is about Henry Schulte—and that is very sad. I am not sure whether you know that some years ago he had a psychiatric break and was in an institution. I did not know it until recently. Now I realize that he has been getting gradually worse for some time. He became much worse after you left and seemed completely unable to pull himself together or do anything, and all of his actions became very queer. Bongi was most kind and considerate and tried to help him, but Henry became quite paranoid and thought Bongi and others were against him. He tried to convince Mary Ellen and Betty that we were dissatisfied with him, and he went to Schwentker and everyone about his injustices, etc. Finally, on the advice of Joan Hampson and others, we decided to let him go. This was very sad.

Yours sincerely,
Lawson Wilkins, MD."

That was a short notice! But my telegraphic answer was an acceptance. This was followed by a frantic rush to obtain an emigration visa: Drs. Wilkins and Samuels sent letters emphasizing that I was needed for the job, and as soon as possible.

A friend from Philadelphia, Mr. Kenneth Skilling, was in Paris at that time and he helped with bank questions. The US Consulate required a Baltimore police certificate, so I wrote to Dr. Wilkins. On December 10, 1952, he answered:

"Dear Claude:

I received your letters of December 10 and 12, concerning the difficulties about your visa. I immediately called Mr. Frank of the Immigration and Naturalization Service. He did not know about the blank, which had been sent to him, but he told me very definitely that all that you needed was a certificate from our Commissioner of Police in Baltimore stating that you had no criminal record. Fortunately, the Commissioner of Police, Col. Beverly Ober is one of my very best friends. I telephoned him about the matter, and he immediately made out the certificate which I am enclosing. I think that this will probably have to be presented at the American Consulate in Paris, and I trust it will clear up the difficulties about your visa. If there are any other problems, please let me know.

As soon as you have made plans concerning your return, please let me hear about them. You must arrange to spend some time in Baltimore. Lucile and I would like to have you stay with us, as you know we have plenty of room. Let me know when you are coming and how long you can stay.

I hope that you receive your Christmas card from us before you leave. Lucile tells me that she did not send it air mail. The Grand Marnier is magic. Under its influence, I could both speak and write French as you may see on the card.

Yours sincerely,
Lawson Wilkins, MD

29

PREPARING FOR THE RETURN TO THE UNITED STATES

After making the decision to go to Salt Lake City, I had to close my affairs in Paris. I disposed of my books and some personal items from my "chambre de bonne" by putting them in pension with my good friend, Colette Bollig. I would recover them upon my return from the USA. At that point, I was still considering returning to France to spend the rest of my life, after my stay in Mormon Country. My knowledge of Mormonism at the time came from the 1921 book written by Pierre Benoit, *Le Lac Salé*. So, I do not exaggerate when I say that my knowledge of Salt Lake City and its university were quite limited. Nonetheless, I looked forward to experiencing a new adventure

I said goodbye to a lot of friends. I spent Christmas with my father in Lens and New Years with my uncle and aunt who had raised me in Rethel. Then, I took the train back to Paris.

On January 10, 1953, I was on a TWA plane flying from Paris to New York with a stop in Shannon, Ireland, and Reykjavik, Iceland. This was a long trip, as jet planes were not in use yet.

30

A FEW DAYS OF FUN IN BALTIMORE (JANUARY 1953)

Iarrived in New York City, Kennedy Airport, took a taxi ride to the Pennsylvania train station and I was on my way to Baltimore. I was exhausted, a little sad to leave family, as well as apprehensive about my job in Utah.

The three-hour ride gave me a chance to ask myself if I had made the right decision. I could have stayed in France, and found a position as a pediatrician in the provincial city of Reims, capital of Champagne and two hours from Paris by train. I would have found a wife and settled down with a nice family. I guess Wilkins had more confidence in my ability than I probably had. I had no easy answer. But then a short taxi ride to 501 Edgevale Road and I was at the Wilkins home. Both Lucile and Lawson were very warm. I had brought gifts, a bottle of Remy Martin Cognac for Lawson and a scarf for Lucile. We had a wonderful supper.

The next day, we had breakfast and I accompanied Lawson to Hopkins. I had fun saying hello to all the people I had met before: the secretaries, Alfred Bongiovanni, Walter Eberlein and George Clayton, the technicians: Mary-Ellen Crafton and Betty Youngblood, Dr. Josephs and Dr. Helen Harrison. This was like returning home.

During my time at the Wilkins home, I had to visit the garden, a pride of Dr. Wilkins. There was not much to see in January, but Lawson showed me the trees behind the house and he discussed his plans for the spring. We talked at length about some of the patients I had met in the previous two years. Mrs. Mahool, the mother of Lucile, came to visit.

But the time passed quickly and I had promised to go to Salt Lake City as fast as I could. So after five days, I had to go back to New York to take my plane. We were late driving to the station for the train to NYC. Dr. Wilkins had insisted that I should take the Baltimore and Ohio train rather than the Pennsylvania train. Unfortunately there was some accident on the way to the station. Lawson drove on the sidewalk to avoid the problem and we made it on time.

Lawson asked me how much money I had with me. He decided that it was not enough and forced me to take two fifty-dollar bills. I promised to keep him posted on my life in Utah. We said good-bye and I was on the train, a little sad and a little scared of what I would find in the "City of the Mormons."

31

TO SALT LAKE CITY

The United Airlines plane I boarded at Kennedy stopped in Denver en route to Salt Lake City. On landing in Salt Lake City, the plane just touched the runway but it roared back its motors and we went back into the air. We were told that there was a problem on the runway. We made a short turn and then tried again to land, this time successfully. When I wrote to Dr. Wilkins, I noted that this incident was frightening and I wondered if it was a bad omen.

Salt Lake City is on the floor of prehistoric Lake Bonneville, caught between the Wasatch Mountains. I found it was blessed with a very bright sun and full of pure air— but not much was going on. The airport was ten minutes from downtown. The streets were amazingly wide and everything was very clean. I explained to Lawson that one has a strange feeling, breathing a little faster, because of the altitude of 1320 meters.

After a short taxi ride, I was passing by the central buildings of the University of Utah. A turn to the right, and we were in front of an austere construction, the medical school. This building included only the basic sciences. On the second floor was the office of the Department of Biochemistry. Here, I was welcomed warmly by the

Figure 24. Leo T. Samuels, Director of the Department of Biochemistry at the University of Utah School of Medicine in Salt Lake City

department secretary, Margerie Riches. Dr. L.T. Samuels (Figure 24) was out of town for a few days, but Margerie, in the most comforting way, took care of making arrangements for a small apartment near the University grounds. She made sure that the place would be affordable. By that time, Dr. John Plager and Robert Martin were in the office. Both offered to drive me to check out my potential apartment. And then we went to see my new home. Everyone was very kind and helpful. I was invited for supper by Hans Reich, a fellow from Switzerland and his wife, Elsa.

The next day, I was introduced to my laboratory, a good-sized room with a central bench, and benches on both sides. At the end of the room, there was a large window and a desk. I was also introduced to my three technicians: Anne Keller, Carma Darley and Patricia Wall. I met a dishwasher, Carl Paul, a good Mormon. Everyone was pleasant and helpful. I explained all this in my letter to Dr. Wilkins. He answered back, stating that he was not surprised by the warm welcome; he knew many people at the University of Utah.

32

PHYSIOLOGY AND PATHOLOGY OF ADRENAL FUNCTION (1953-1955)

I rapidly learned that the Utah group had pioneered the assay of cortisol in human blood: the Nelson-Samuels method. The new tool appeared to have involved most of the clinical departments of the hospital: Drs. C.H. Hardin Branch and Eugene Bliss in Psychiatry, Drs. Frank Tyler, Avery Sandburg, Harold Brown, Roy Slaunwhite and JZ Bowers in Medicine, Dr. Vincent Kelly in Pediatrics, Dr. Holmstrom in Gynecology, Drs. John Plager, Kris Eik Nes and Hans Reich in Biochemistry and Dr. A.B. French in Physiology. All this activity appeared to be directed by Dr. Leo Samuels. Dr. Wilkins was informed, as I reported to him that we studied the diurnal variation of cortisol in men and monkeys, the effects of surgical and psychological stress on cortisol secretion, the effects of ACTH under various clinical conditions, the effects of insulin, histamine and bacterial pyrogens, the response to electroconvulsant therapy and whole body irradiation.

I sent the prepublication papers of the group to Dr. Wilkins and he gave his comments. In three years, I was an author on twenty scientific papers.

I had fun with the study of psychological stress. The subjects were medical students who were taking their final oral exam in Medicine given by Dr. Maxwell Wintrobe. He had designed the special tube for determination of hematocrit when he was at Hopkins before becoming the Chief of Medicine at Utah. He had the reputation of being very demanding and the students were anxious about his exam. So, we took three blood samples two to three weeks before the exam and one immediately before and after the exam. Psychologists determined the level of anxiety of each student. The results showed no correlation between the anxiety and the degree of increase of cortisol; so much for psychological stress and cortisol response. But, in most cases, there was some increase of levels following the exam, demonstrating the potency of an oral exam with Dr. Wintrobe.

33

MY SOCIAL LIFE AT THE UNIVERSITY OF UTAH MEDICAL SCHOOL

When Lawson wrote that he hoped that I did not regret following his advice, I had to tell him that everybody in the Department of Biochemistry was very kind and pleasant. I explained that all the staff, technicians and secretaries had a very cordial relationship. Everyone worked very hard including Saturdays and parts of Sundays. But on Wednesdays at noon, the laboratory closed down for skiing! I understood that starting early in the fall and through late in spring, this was the thing to do. Wednesday had been chosen because the cost of the lift was one-third of that on weekends, and there were much fewer skiers on the slopes.

Figure 25. Our group in the Department of Biochemistry
with Mrs.Samuels in front on a knee. (1954)

I was told that I had to learn to ski. Hans Reich gave me a pair of skis. Someone else provided the pants and jacket and a third, the gloves and poles. On the first Wednesday, at noon, two or three cars would be ready. Everyone had a sandwich to eat en route. (Figure 25)

I was given lessons on "how to fall," which was apparently very important. Then I was put on a seat of the lift and taken to the top of the slope. From there, I looked at the bottom, but was advised that I could snow plow, going down from one side of the slope to the other. Margery Riches was kind and was there to pick me up when I fell. After several falls, I managed to reach the inn at the bottom, where I was congratulated by my friends.

The beauty of the Wasatch Mountains of Utah is incredible. I explained to Lawson the importance of skiing. Several of the medical staff, like Dr. Cartright, went in spring to evaluate the amount of snow in various locations in order to predict how much snow would melt to furnish water for the irrigation of the cultures of the farmers.

Also, on July 4, young skiers go to the top of mountains surrounding Salt Lake City and ski down at night with a torch in hand—a beautiful spectacle!

While I did learn to ski, I was not very good at it. In the spring of 1954, the group went to Snow Basin. It was a beautiful sunny day, but it was icy on the slopes. I fell and broke my left fibula. Hans Reich, who saw me fall, decided that I was fine, so he went down with the rest of my friends. As it was noon, the lift stopped running, everybody had their sandwiches, while I sat halfway down the slope, unable to move. Eventually, the lift restarted, the ski patrol picked me up and Dr. Samuels's wife, Barbara, who was part of our group of skiers took me to the emergency room in Salt Lake to obtain a cast. For a few days, I stayed at the Samuels'.

When I was able to move with a walking cast and a cane, I went back to work at the medical school. Young students that I did not know would salute me with, "How is your skiing these days?"

The next year, I was quite willing to pass on skiing, but because I was being called a quitter, I went skiing again. I have to admit that I was extremely careful and I never skied again after returning to the East Coast.

After skiing, there was usually a visit to a Mexican restaurant for tacos and enchiladas.

During the summer, the trips to the mountains were for picnics with a fire for cooking hot dogs and marshmallows.

Part of my indoctrination was that I had to attend concerts. The Salt Lake City Orchestra, directed by the renowned Maurice Abravanel, was quite excellent. The Mormon was an impressive group of wonderful singers. Many Mormons competed to become part of the choir. Verdi's "Requiem" by the orchestra and the choir was incomparable to anything I had heard before or since. However, one trouble with the concerts was that the acoustics of the hall were rather poor. The oval shape of the hall distorted the sound. In only two parts of the auditorium could you hear the music just once, everywhere else there was an annoying echo.

The University Theater was another function I was told I must attend. The students were good actors. The production of *Julius Cesar* was almost too much to take. Hordes of Roman soldiers surged throughout the theater, dressed with their short skirts, carrying lances, and epees.

The football games between the University of Utah and Brigham Young University were a heated rivalry. Our entire department always was eager to cheer for U of U! I was amazed that some of the people who attended the games drank from metal flasks (probably scotch). As Lawson knew Mormons do not drink any alcohol, on my visit to Baltimore, he suggested I have an extra glass of liquor to catch up for the dry spell.

One time, I was visited by Jim and Sylvia Tait, the British researchers who first isolated aldosterone. I invited them to dinner at the best restaurant in town at the Hotel Utah. I had bought a bottle of good, expensive French wine from the state-run alcohol distribution center, the only place where alcohol could be purchased. I knew that the restaurant would permit wine in glasses, but the bottle had to be kept under the table.

At the appropriate time, I asked the waiter for a corkscrew. He blushed and said he did not have one. He went back to the kitchen and eventually came back, but with no corkscrew. So, I explained to the Taits that I would see if I could find one in a drug store. Having no success. I kept the bottle between my legs throughout the dinner. Jim never let me forget this fiasco and his first words, whenever he saw me, were to inquire whether I had kept the habit of keeping a corked bottle of wine under the table each time I went to a restaurant. When I told Dr. Wilkins about this ordeal, he did not find it funny.

34

THE CIBA FOUNDATION:
LONDON (APRIL 1954)

I wrote Dr. Wilkins that I had been invited to speak at the Colloquium on Endocrinology (Vol. 8) organized by Dr. Gordon Wolstenholme and Miss Margaret Cameron to be held in London. The colloquium was entitled "The Human Adrenal Cortex." I told him that Dr. Frank Taylor was going to present our work on the effects of epinephrine on the metabolism of 17-hydroxy-corticosteroids in humans. I added that I was going to present my work on "Adreno-cortical Function and Plasmic 17-ketosteroids in Man."

Figure 26. The CIBA Foundation in London. From left: Ian Bush, Claude Migeon and Kenneth Savard. (April 1954)

Lawson answered that he was also going to that meeting and would give a paper in collaboration with Al Bongiovanni, George Clayton, Mel Grumbach and Jud Van Wyk on the steroid abnormalities in and treatment of congenital adrenal hyperplasia.

Bongiovanni had shown that their patients had an excessive secretion of 17-hydroxyprogesterone and progesterone in addition to the adrenal androgens.

Lawson and I made plans to see each other in London. I took a plane from Salt Lake to New York and then the TWA plane to London, with stops in Reykjavik, Iceland, and Shannon, Ireland.

The senior investigators, including Lawson, were accommodated at the Ciba Foundation, 41 Portland Place. I had a hotel close to the Foundation, sharing a room with Dr. Ian Bush, a great friend. Drs. Ken Savard (Figure 26) and Claude Giroud of Montreal were next door. Several other young investigators were with us as well.

I had a long conversation with Lawson. He told me that he was very pleased with his present fellows. Bongiovanni had worked with Liebermann in New York and had fascinating data that explained the pathophysiology of CAH. In addition, Grumbach and Van Wyk were working very hard.

There were several special meals at the meeting with toasts "To the Queen," which Dr. Wilkins loved.

The scientists who contributed were the world experts in the field. First, there were the studies of aldosterone: Wettstein and Neher of Basel, Dr. Venning from Montreal, Sylvia Simpson and James Tait who had just isolated aldosterone, Dr. Gaunt from the United States, and Dr. Prader from Zurich.

Then there were the "clinicians" like Lawson, Drs. George Thorn and Andrea Prader.

Dr. Frank Taylor did a great job in presenting our data and my own paper was well received but with many questions raised about the testicular androgen testosterone.

Peggy Cameron, one of the conference organizers, had visited us in Salt Lake City, and it was fun to see her again. I had a chance to talk to many of the attendees, and it was very instructive.

A bus was taking some of us to the airport. I had to say goodbye very quickly to Lawson before heading back to Salt Lake City and the laboratory with my laboratory assistants.

35

AN IMPORTANT VISIT TO CHILDREN'S HOSPITAL OF HARVARD (SEPTEMBER 1955)

In 1955, John Crigler, who had been a colleague my first year in Baltimore, was now settling into his new position as the head of the Pediatric Endocrine Clinic at Harvard Children's Hospital. We had talked about me joining him and establishing a hormone research laboratory. He was very anxious to have me, and invited me to Boston to discuss my needs. I also was asked to give a lecture, which was a little intimidating. As I was walking toward the conference room, Dr. Charles Janeway, the chief of Boston Children's Hospital and a wonderful person, noticed my nervousness. He told me that he always had to go to the bathroom to empty his bladder and wondered if that was my problem, too. We both went to the men's room and urinated together. This common humanity relieved my apprehension and my lecture went very well.

My talk was followed by a visit to the Jimmy Fund Cancer Research Building, the domain of Dr. Sidney Farber. Dr. Janeway told me that I had to be introduced to him, and that we would have lunch together.

We went to the top floor of the building, the place where Dr. Farber had established his library. All the books on the shelves were hiding behind wooden panels, and a table was set for four people. I was introduced to Dr. Farber, whom I knew was an important decider about new faculty at Children's Hospital.

Then, the maid (cook) brought a plate of chicken to Dr. Janeway, another plate to John Crigler and one to me. Finally she returned with a huge steak, and presented it to Dr. Farber who explained, "Too bad, I cannot eat chicken." The memory of his special lunch has remained with me for all these years. When I told Lawson about it, he had a big laugh.

After I had gone through all the steps required of the visit, I took the train back to Baltimore to discuss my plans with Dr. Wilkins. Both John Crigler and Dr. Janeway had given me encouragement. We discussed what I would need for my research and everything seemed to be acceptable.

Because I had not told Wilkins of the major reason for my Boston visit, he was a little shocked when I told him that I was thinking of joining John Crigler. He asked, "Why don't you come back with me in Baltimore instead?" I answered that I had believed that was not possible. I told Lawson that my research would require a laboratory room with a special spark-proof hood and also a small room with thirty-seven degrees Celsius constant temperature for paper chromatography using the Bush system. Lawson interrupted, suggesting that I stay a couple of days to discuss the possibility of filling my requirements. The next morning, Lawson, brought me to one of the engineers of the hospital. We first went to the fifth floor of Harriet Lane home to check on space. They identified a small room that could serve as the thirty-seven degree Celsius constant temperature room for chromatography. The old lab in the middle of the floor could be equipped with a hood, and its working bench could support cabinets that could be used for glassware. For an office, we found a broom closet, nine by four feet, with a sterilizer at one end.

There was a lot of work to be done to make that space workable, but the engineer said that it was feasible. However, the matter of cost did not come into discussion.

Before I left, Dr. Wilkins asked me to hold up my decision for Boston until he could get some information he needed. Back for two weeks in Salt Lake City, I got a phone call from Lawson; the work could be done, it would take three months. Then he asked if I would come back to Hopkins. After one more week, I called Lawson to tell him I accepted his offer and would come back in October of 1955.

36

RETURN TO BALTIMORE
(OCTOBER 1955)

The friendships I made with my colleagues at the University of Utah were memorable. The social life was wonderful. There were group trips to Sun Valley and the Grand Teton Mountains, to Yellow State Park with a stay at the Inn. The expeditions to the southern parks including Mesa Verde were a lot of fun, as were trips to Reno and San Francisco for meetings. Despite all this, I had a feeling of being isolated. San Francisco is 750 miles from Salt Lake City and the East Coast is 1700 miles away. So, after three wonderful years in Utah, I was ready to move back to the East Coast. I thought I was going to Harvard, but I ended up at Hopkins again.

Having acquired lots of things to carry with me, I decided to buy a second-hand Chevrolet. It was not a beautiful car, but I believed that it would carry all my junk and books. I also filled up a large trunk with my belongings and shipped it by train to Baltimore. It was so heavy that I managed to rupture a dorsal spinal disk. Bob Martin helped me to move it to the station.

There were several suppers and parties to say goodbye to the many colleagues, coworkers in the lab, the Samuels, and the lovely Wasatch Mountains.

But eventually, I took to the road. Lytt Gardner had organized a meeting in Syracuse, New York by. So, I planned to drive to Lake Ontario before heading south to Baltimore.

I was quite naïve about the distances in the USA. The way to go was simple: Route 80 to south Chicago and then Route 90. It took me several days with a stop at Cheyenne. I did not realize that the state of Nebraska was so long—a very monotonous trek with hills after hills. I used my radio for company but on Saturday, there was only college football. I had to listen to one game twice, as it was repeated later in the day. But finally, I made it to Syracuse.

There, I found all my old friends from the East Coast: Dr. Wilkins, Bongiovanni, Crigler, Eberlein and the whole psychohormonal group: John Money, the Hampsons and fellows. Lytt Gardner was now director of Pediatric Endocrinology at Syracuse University. I was glad to see all of them.

The meeting was very exciting. John Money was very prominent in all the discussions relating to sexual abnormalities.

After the meeting, Dr. Wilkins told me to take Route 81 to Harrisburg and then 83 to Hopkins, and invited me to stay at his home, until I could get resettled in Baltimore.

Searching for an apartment of my own, I quickly found one on the second floor of a private home on Schenley Road. One entered the apartment through the living room. There was a large bedroom, with a small balcony, a very small kitchen, and a tiny bathroom. It was furnished but minimally. There were some red plastic curtains at the windows, which gave a bad impression at night when my lights were on. I bought a secondhand radio and this is where I lived for the next five years.

37

BACK TO HOPKINS

I enjoyed finding colleagues who I already knew. The fellows were Jud Van Wyk and Melvin Grumbach. John Money was an old friend. The technicians were still Mary-Ellen Crafton and Betty Youngblood. I was then an Assistant Professor.

At the north end of the fifth floor, I found Dr. Victor Najjar, who worked in the same space as Dr. James Gamble and Dr. Jim Sidbury. In Boston, I had met Gamble's father, an expert in electrolyte equilibrium in newborns and infants. Both Jims offered to help get my trunk at the station. Jim Sidbury was a real Southerner from North Carolina. A real friend, he called me "Cousin Claude" and I called him "Cousin Jim."

Dr. Wilkins told me that I had to pay a visit to the head of the Department of Pediatrics, Dr. Schwentker. So, I made an appointment with the secretary. When I entered the office, I noticed immediately a vertical wood stick on the side of the desk of Dr. Schwentker with a magnificent, huge bird of many colors. I shook hands with the pleasant-looking man across his desk and he asked me to sit down in front of him. At that point, there was a big noise of feathers flying up in the air. And as Dr. Schwenker sat down, the parrot flew to rest on his right shoulder. I was very perplexed when the Chief of Pediatrics welcomed me into the department. I was not quite sure if I had this conversation with the man or the bird. I said thank you quickly and left his office, flabbergasted. Of course, I reported my adventure to Lawson, who smiled a little and told me about Dr. Schwentker's struggles with alcohol abuse.

I also found several French-speaking doctors at the Baltimore City Hospital (now called Bayview). In Medicine, there was Ives Boennec and Francis Bazin with his wife Jeanine, a nurse. In surgery, there was Felicien Steichen from

Luxembourg, the nephew of the very popular photographer Edward Steichen, the author of the famous exhibit "The Family of Man." Their group decided that as I was a little older, I was to be their "uncle" and they called me "Tonton Claude." At that point, I had obtained the family designations of both "cousin" and "tonton."

Not everything can go as anticipated. My poor old Chevy had crossed the USA brilliantly but it expired shortly after arriving in Baltimore. I asked a mechanic to look at it but his diagnosis was terrible. I would have to change the motor completely. Basically, the car stayed in front of my apartment, incapable of moving. At that stage, I did not have the cash to buy another car. Lawson decided that he could make a little detour and drive me to and from my apartment on Schenley Road every day. This started a series of twice daily twenty-five minute discussions with Dr. Wilkins.

38

DAILY COMMUTES WITH DR. WILKINS

It turned out that the daily trip from my apartment to Hopkins Hospital in Dr. Wilkins's car was a great way to have very personal conversations.

CONVERSATION 1: DR. WILKINS AND HIS FAMILY

One day, Lawson would start talking about his family life, how Lucile was good to him and tolerant of his idiosyncrasies. She had been very supportive at the time of the accident and death of Skippy. She had encouraged him to go back to carpentry. She helped him to go on his gardening, which was very comforting to him.

I learned that Lawson was quite fond of his mother-in-law, Mrs. Mahool. However, he did not understand how a conservative person like her could vote Democratic instead of Republican like him, just because she was a Southerner. He was not as fond of his brother-in-law, Tom Mahoul, who having never married, still lived with his mother.

Dr. Wilkins would tell me that Skippy went to Gilman School but had some problems with schoolwork. Yet, he was a very attractive young man, very good in sports and had a great deal of social grace. He probably had a mild learning disability. Although Lawson thought Skippy might not be able to make it in medical school, he thought his son would have been great in business or law. His daughter, Betsy, was an excellent student but she was not interested in medicine as a career.

CONVERSATION 2: MY EDUCATION IN FRANCE (1936-1950)

On one occasion, Lawson wanted to know about my schooling in France. I told him that it had been quite complex. First, I went to Ecole Carnot in Lens (Pas de Calais) where I was a good enough student but did not work very hard. After my mother died, I went to live with my mother's sister who had been married ten years with no children. So, she and my uncle who was also my godfather were pleased to take my brother Michel and me. Her husband was my godfather, but he was also director of the small college of Rethel (Ardennes). My aunt played piano and taught music at the school. The move changed my attitude toward schoolwork. I continually competed for first of the class with a child named Guy Voillemin. Then in 1939, the Second World War started. We were obliged to move from Rethel to our evacuation site, close to La Rochelle at Fontenay-le-Comte (Vendée) where I went to the College François Viete.

In the fall of 1940, the Germans had invaded France and Rethel (Ardennes) was in a "zone interdite," but because we lived there, we were permitted to return. When we arrived, we found that many houses of the city had been destroyed. Fortunately, our house survived; there was only a hole on one side above the garage that was later repaired. However, a German officer was living in our house. When we rang the bell, a soldier opened the door, and called his officer. We discussed our problem with the officer who agreed to let us in. But he would take the salon (our living room) as his office, the dining room for his bedroom and he demanded access to our kitchen. This was an awkward situation for six months until the officer was called to the Russian front. Lawson wanted to know how we could live with the German solider. I explained that compromises were necessary, if we wanted a roof over our heads.

For school, I had to go to the Lycée de Reims and I lived the first year with a large family in their big house. The winter of 1939-1940 was absolutely miserable and I can say that I know what it means to be hungry. The harvests had been lost, the cattle destroyed. We had tickets, twenty-five grams of meat per week, no milk and no bread. By the spring of 1940, people began to use their gardens to cultivate potatoes. We had a hen in our garden, which gave us an egg from time to time.

In 1941, I passed the first part of the baccalaureate and the second part in 1942. I rented a room from a very nice lady, Madame Moraux, who lived with her twelve-year-old grandson, Christian. From our third-floor apartment on

44, Rue Jean Jacques Rousseau, I first saw bombs falling from allied planes on the airport of Reims! It was strange.

In the summer of 1942, I had to decide what my career would be. I was very good in mathematics and considered competing for what the French call "les grande écoles" like Polytechnique. But I thought that maybe I was not good enough. My best friend, Huber Pautet, felt strongly about medicine, so I decided to do it, too. Reims had a school for the preparatory year, "physique, chemistry, biology" or PCB. At the end of that year, there was an exam and only half the students could start the first year of medicine. At that time, Reims provided only the first two years of medical studies.

On January 1, 1945, after the "liberation," I was called into the army, where I ran an infirmary on the front in Alsace.

As the armistice was signed on September 1, 1945, I was permitted to go back to school for my third year at the Medical School of Paris. We rotated through various hospitals in the city. I took my Pediatrics rotations at the Hopital Necker-Enfants Malades, Rue de Sévres. My mentors were Dr. Julien Huber, Soterios Briskas and Robert Debré. This rotation convinced me to specialize in Pediatrics. In 1949, however, I spent a short rotation on a ward (about twenty beds) full of children with tuberculous meningitis for whom no specific treatment was available. This shocked me. At that time, I began to realize that doctors had to do research to solve such medical problems.

Of interest, at that time, I attended girls with Turner Syndrome. I obtained some of my information from your papers, Dr. Wilkins. I have to admit that I had no idea that I would work someday with the smart physician who had published these papers.

Lawson Wilkins explained how he was able to better understand the pathophysiology of the Turner Syndrome with the help of Dr. Howard Jones, the gynecologist, he found that these girls had no ovaries. He also studied their multiple congenital malformations including heart, kidneys, webbed neck, and poor stature and growth. It was strange for me to remember the time when I was reading the paper of Wilkins L. and Fleischmann W. of 1944 on "Ovarian Agenesis" while seeing such patients in Paris. This great physician was now sitting next to me and was my mentor driving me home.

CONVERSATION 3: DR. ERNEST SCHAFFNER AND THE FRENCH RESISTANCE (1939-1945)

On one of our trips, Lawson wanted to know about the French Resistance in the Second World War. I told him that I was not officially a member but I worked with Dr. Ernest Schaffner, a forty-year-old friend of my family who I found out later was in charge of a resistance medical network in the region.

Dr. Schaffner was born in 1901, in Strasbourg, as a German citizen since Alsace had been annexed by Germany after the war of 1870. His father was the conservateur of the beautiful cathedral of Strasbourg. He spoke an Alsatian dialect, but also knew French and German. Since 1918, Alsace/Lorraine again belonged to France. During his years of medical school, he contracted tuberculosis but recovered after several stays in a sanatorium. In the late '20s, he was named Chief hysician of the "Dispensaire antituberculeux d'hygiene sociale" of the coal mines of Lens/Liévin. He organized a hospital and several infirmaries in the region. He was a physiologist who studied silicosis of the coal miners. Many had tuberculosis as well.

In the summer of 1943 and 1944, Dr. Schaffner accepted me to work with him. He was willing to state that he needed me, and that avoided my being sent to work in Germany. He had known my mother and was a friend of my father. I followed him everywhere as he worked at the hospital, the dispensary, and making home visits. There was not any real treatment or antibiotics at the time. Dr. Schaffner used pneumothorax and followed the effects on the lungs by X-ray. This was successful in a few cases of tuberculosis but not for silicosis.

When I went to work with him, he had been in practice for many years. By that time, he had lost several fingers of his left hand and one finger on the right. He was a victim of the X-ray, like its inventor, Dr. Marie Curie.

Now, he was using gloves for protection and made me do the same. We visited the dispensary in the morning, and after that the hospital where patients were cared for by nuns. Sister Martine would have a sandwich and cup of coffee for us.

Dr. Schaffner was adored by the patients, their families and the nurses. They called him the "Apostle of Lens." When we went to a café for a drink, he would never be charged for it. At the patients' homes, there was always something for us to eat or drink. The devotion of Dr. Schaffner to his patients was equaled by the devotion of the patients to their doctor, whom they saw as a father.

Because he spoke German, he could communicate easily with the German authorities. He was respected by the Kommendantur, as he was very important to the healthcare of the coal miners, as the Germans used the coal for their industries.

I also admired Dr. Schaffner and asked if I could help him in any way. One day he asked me if I could deliver some letters in Paris because he did not trust the post office. I accepted rather innocently, not realizing that I had become a "carrier." I would be given a ticket for the train to Paris, and I would deliver two or three letters each time. When I was in Paris, after the delivery was made, I would visit my cousins Jeanine, Fabienne and Edmée, who all worked at the Service des Eaux de la Ville de Paris. I thought this was fun, not realizing that if I were caught, I could be sent to a concentration camp. Dr. Wilkins wanted to know if I was scared. I guess I looked fairly young and innocent when I was twenty years old and in fact, did not know what I was doing.

CONVERSATION 4: THE ENGLISH PILOT AT THE FRENCH BROTHEL AMONG GERMAN SOLDIERS (AUGUST 1943)

Another story I had to tell Dr. Wilkins about was my other experience in the French Underground. At the end of one day, Dr. Schaffner told the nurse and me that we had to go immediately to the brothel.

I should give some explanation: I knew that a certain café was a house of prostitution. Like everyone else in town, the madame in charge knew Dr. Schaffner. The prostitutes were followed at the Dispensaire d' Hygiene Sociale. This is where I became an expert in taking blood samples and infusing IV therapy for syphilis.

When we entered, we were in a large room, full of smoke with tables and German soldiers and French girls drinking at the tables. The madame took us into a little room, closed the door and asked us what she was to do with the English pilot that had just arrived.

As it turned out, the brothel was the place to which the underground would send allied airmen who had been on their way to bomb Germany when they were forced to parachute into Holland and Belgium.

Dr. Wilkins wanted to know what we did with the English pilot. I was the only one in our group who had had four years of English classes, so I was the one to check on the man. I was also asked to check his underwear to make sure that they did not have German labels. I could verify that the labels were from Utrecht, Holland.

I was told that the man would be sent to the next relay, on his way to Portugal and then on to England. I have no idea if he made it.

Dr. Wilkins and I further discussed the occupation of France by Germany. The French tried to survive the best they could. The madame and the prostitutes would entertain German soldiers. Yet, at the same time, they were involved in the Resistance. This was hard to explain but it was a fact of life.

Dr. Schaffner did not run into trouble with the German authorities, which was something of a miracle. After the war, he went to visit his friend, Dr. Albert Schweitzer, the Nobel Peace Prize winner, in his renowned Hospital in Lambaréné (Gabon). He died at sixty-five years of age, the result of radiation exposure. Lawson agreed with me that Dr. Schaffner lived an unusual life.

CONVERSATION 5: DR. WILKINS AND WORLD WAR I

On one of our trips, Lawson told me how he had been involved in World War I (Figure 5). When the USA entered the war, the Hopkins Medical School decided to send to Europe a base hospital consisting of staff members of the school along with medical student volunteers.

In May of 1917, a large group of medical personnel was formed under the direction of Dr. J.M.T. Finney as Base Hospital #18. The group was made up of physicians with all specialties represented. There were thirty-two third-year medical students including Lawson, pharmacists, nurses, physical therapists, dentists, administrators, laboratory technicians, secretaries, carpenters and cooks. In addition to all these people they sent along a large amount of supplies including beds, surgical equipment and drugs. Base Hospital #18 boarded a ship in New Jersey and sailed to France, on June 14, 1917.

The conditions on the ship were not the best, and Lawson reported that much of the personnel became seasick. There were so many people on the boat that they could not come on the deck together. They had to rotate in order to get fresh air. Because of the presence of German submarines, the boat took a torturous route that took fourteen days before arriving at St. Nazaire, the French harbor at the estuary of the Loire River.

They were rapidly moved to Savenay about ten kilometers north of St. Nazaire; there was a large hospital base there. Savenay was a lovely little town and the native French people were very friendly. Lawson had been able to travel a little north of Savenay, visiting Brittany, which he loved.

After a month at Savenay, they took an eleven-hour train ride to reach the Vosges in Lorraine. They debarked at Bazailles sur Meuse, a village of farms with about five hundred inhabitants. The Base Hospital #18 settled near the Chateau de Bazailles: this was a one thousand-bed unit that opened on July 26, 1917. Six other Bases, each of about one thousand beds, were also established on both sides of the Meuse River.

The base, according to Lawson, was almost four miles south of Neufchâteau, a small town of seven thousand inhabitants. The country was very lovely with the Vosges hills and beautiful woods.

Lawson and his schoolmates played the roles of interns, anesthetists and lab technicians. However, they also had to do all sorts of work like cleaning the latrines and helping in the kitchens.

They cared for a lot of sick soldiers as well as many wounded men. They received casualties from various fronts: Verdun was seventy miles north, Nancy forty miles east. The "Second Battle of the Marne" and the Bois Belleayre near Fère-en-Tardenois and Reims was not far. At the medical center, they had fifty thousand patients and eight hundred deaths.

The American army sustained very heavy losses, a total of 50,000 men— most of them killed at the front—and 200,000 wounded. Of course, the total Allied losses were about 2,500,000 men—the same number as the dead Germans/Austrians.

Lawson wanted me to know that from Savenay, he had gone fifteen miles north to Vannes, a lovely old city on the coast. There he was invited by French people to come and participate in their meal. Lawson was willing to say that there were also three lovely young ladies. He did not go into further detail, nor did I request more details. But it is a fact that Dr. Wilkins had become a lover of French culture.

CONVERSATION 6: THE "HOUSES OF TOLERANCE" AT SAVENAY DURING WORLD WAR I

On another trip, Lawson told me about one unusual aspect of the Franco-American alliance. The city of Savenay was close to the harbor of St. Nazaire and it had many "houses of prostitution" open to sailors and visitors. The hygiene of these places was very poor and there were numerous cases of venereal disease reported.

After the debarkment of the first groups of American troops, the military authority became concerned and General Pershing made the houses of tolerance off-limits for the American soldiers. It would appear that the mayor of the city complained. It is said that it went to the President of France, Georges Clemenceau. After long and arduous discussions, the control of designated houses would be given to American medical authorities.

I asked how this sexual conflict was resolved at the levels of the high authorities. Lawson was not sure. When Base Hospital #18 was closed on January 20, 1919, Dr. Wilkins returned to Savenay. He thinks that there had been a solution to the problem.

On February 20, 1919, the personnel of Base Hospital #18, including Wilkins, was back in New Jersey. Lawson was trying to find a position of intern in the United States. Despite that late date for finding a position, he managed to find a place at Yale!

CONVERSATION 7: HOW LAWSON WILKINS CAME TO DEVELOP THE FIELD OF PEDIATRIC ENDOCRINOLOGY

On September 1, 1939, World War II started in Europe. The USA joined the conflict after the attack on Pearl Harbor on December 11, 1941. Wilkins said he was too old to join the army. He became very busy, covering the practice of other pediatricians. His routine was early home visits to patients. Then it was the hospitals, both Hopkins and Union Memorial Hospitals. This was followed by his practice at his office, 1014 St. Paul Street. He finished his days very late; Lucile would prepare his supper, and he claimed that he needed a stiff nightcap, usually rye alcohol, to carry him to sleep until early the next day.

Dr. Edwards Park, chief of Pediatrics at Hopkins, had offered him a full-time position that Lawson refused via letter on December 17, 1943, saying, "For years, I have found myself torn between the things I would like to do and those I have to do." Lawson felt a duty to his practice and often at night he would consider the problems of the research clinician.

On January 15, 1944, Dr. Wilkins was seeing patients at Union Memorial when a nurse came to tell him that his son was in the hospital, victim of a car accident. Lawson rushed to Skippy's side, but found him dead. This was a terrible shock!

I think that horrible accident helped him to accept the position of Associate Professor in 1946, offered by Dr. Park's successor, Dr. Francis Schwentker. At this time, he started seriously collecting data on pediatric endocrine patients. During the following four years, Lawson built the foundation of his famous book *The Diagnosis and Treatment of Endocrine Disorders in Childhood and Adolescence*. It was published by Charles C. Thomas in 1950, thus beginning the new field of pediatric clinical research.

CONVERSATION 8: THE END OF DAILY RIDES WITH LAWSON

Eventually, I figured out the means to pay for a new car. Dr. Wilkins advised me not to buy a secondhand car. He thought that a Chevrolet would be a good deal, and I took his advice.

Dr. Wilkins knew the manager of the local Chevrolet dealership. He managed to get me a low price on my new car and even some money for my broken car. Of course, my new transportation made life much easier for both Lawson and me.

This was marvelous. Unfortunately, we lost the opportunity to have personal conversations twice daily. However, I still went with Dr. Wilkins to the many lectures that he gave at the Naval Hospital and National Institutes of Health in Bethesda, the Baltimore City Hospital and Union Memorial Hospital. Lawson was in great demand and very generous with his time, but he liked to have company and it was me!

39

SOCIAL LIFE IN BALTIMORE

D r. Wilkins loved parties and Lucile was very accommodating. While he was temporary Director of the Department of Pediatrics after Dr. Schwentker's death, he had parties for the house-staff at his home, which took place at least twice a year, at Christmas and in the summer. These occasions for lots of food and even more drinking. I remember an occasion when Lawson had to take a nap in the grass of the backyard. But before that point, there was a lot of singing; one member of the house-staff played his guitar and a good time was had by all.

During the winter, there was opera at Lyric Theater. I was invited on several occasions. For the opera, Lawson would smoke as it was a social occasion.

As much as Lawson liked Rigoletto and Carmen, he loved the Gilbert and Sullivan operettas. I also was a member of the party and after the show, we had to review the major songs before separating for sleep. Often, he managed to bring up the fact that Skippy loved that specific song and that he had a better voice than his father.

On Sundays during the summer there were trips to the Chesapeake Bay. Dr. Wilkins had a small boat, about eleven feet long, that he manipulated like a real captain. I think that Lawson had cruising vacations with some friends using a large Chesapeake oyster workboat. These two week adventures, I had been told were a lot of fun.

The little sailboat that Lawson shared with me was a miniature dinghy, but Lucile, Betsy and I would receive orders from our "Captain." After a while, Lucile would get the bag with food: fried chicken, potato salad, cucumbers and cold tea. After returning to the dock, there would be a swim, songs and a more vigorous drink prior to the return home. (Figure 27, 28)

Figure 27. The Wilkins family with the Captain of the sailboat. (1955)

Figure 28. Lucile, Lawson and Betsy Wilkins after a swim. (1955)

In July of 1958, the Wilkins family took a three-week vacation on Cape Cod. I went to join them for a few days. The chalet was right on the beach. We swam, went fishing and at night, we played very serious games of bridge. I was the partner of Mrs. Mahool, who was a very smart player. The team of Lawson and Lucile never won, and Lawson was most unhappy. An extra glass of rye alcohol was necessary to console him. A compensation for Lawson was I could give him news of the patients he had left in Baltimore ten days before who I had seen the day before I arrived.

The winter of 1958, Lawson told me he was going with Lucile to Bethlehem, Pennsylvania, to see Emilie, his sister. I was invited to join them. The main attraction was the yearly concert by a fantastic choral and orchestral group at the Moravian church. The program was all Bach, an exceptional occasion. As the local inhabitants were mainly German immigrants, the songs were in German. The concert lived up to the high expectations that Lawson had set for it. It was absolutely magnificent. On the whole, it was very impressive!

I must not forget gardening. This was an important recreation for Lawson. He thought that I did not take enough exercise and he would invite me to come to help him. There was grass to cut, bushes to trim, flowers to plant. It was also an occasion to have a talk with the neighbor, Mr. Allnutt. And of course, as it was hot, we had to have a drink. Lucile would always find some food to go with drinks and we had a lot of fun.

40

REUNION OF MEMBERS OF
THE CLASS OF 1918 OF
JOHNS HOPKINS MEDICAL SCHOOL

On the occasion of their class reunion dinner, Dr. Hugh Morgan from White Bridge, Tennessee, gave the following address:

In recognition of the essential roles Wilkins played in the United States Army in World War I, certain facts should be recorded at this Hopkins dinner honoring Lawson.

Wilkins was the youngest in years and in heart of the thirty-two intrepid soldiers recruited by the Hopkins Base Hospital #18 from the class of 1918. This unique recruitment benefitted enormously the Baltimore residue of the class since it removed a large number of highly talented but odd and difficult characters. It also benefited Base Hospital #18 by providing it with, at one and the same time, military and academic personnel capable of becoming bathers, delousers, bedpan hustlers, duck shooters, grave diggers and honey dippers. By on-the-job training, Wilkins eventually qualified as "expert" in each of these assignments. By his own admission he surpassed the other students in his performance and devotion to duty. Because of this, he achieved almost immediately the military grade of private first class, and furthermore, he was successful in retaining this title, without demotion, throughout his entire career as a student-soldier. All of his classmates agree that wherever he was and in whatever assignment he functioned, Wilkins worked incessantly and successfully.

Our remaining observations have to do with Dr. Lawson Wilkins, Professor of Pediatrics, the Johns Hopkins University.

The class of 1918 recognizes and proudly acclaims Lawson Wilkins as, far and away, its most distinguished member. Clinician, clinical investigator, teacher and author, a professor in his own superb and inimitable manner and, therefore, in the true Hopkins tradition.

On this memorable occasion Lawson Wilkins's classmates acclaim him and wish for him many more productive happy years.

41

DR. JOHN EAGER HOWARD: A COLLEAGUE, FRIEND AND PHYSICIAN OF LAWSON WILKINS

It is important to introduce Dr. Howard when writing about Dr. Wilkins. Dr. Howard represents the aristocracy of Maryland. His ancestor was a general in the Revolutionary War; the statue of General John Eager Howard on horseback is placed right in the middle of Mount Vernon Square in Baltimore City. Dr. Howard reports that on one occasion, his friends put him onto the statue, and he had to explain to the intervening policeman that the statue was of his ancestor. (Figure 29)

Howard lived in a lovely house in Hunt Valley. He was a professor in the Department of Medicine, and was chief of the adult Endocrine Clinic. He held a weekly clinical conference in the Hurd Hall Auditorium, where adult and pediatric patients with difficult or rare diagnoses were presented with Dr. Howard directing the show and tell.

Figure 29. The Endocrine Society Meeting, Atlantic City, NJ. from left: Lawson Wilkins, Douglas Hubble and John Eager Howard. (June 1-4, 1955)

The audience consisted of approximately one hundred physicians. The residents who presented the patients were intimidated by Dr. Howard, and tried hard to be complete and clear. If not, Dr. Howard would be very critical and ridicule the presenters who made mistakes.

One day, I was on the elevator with Dr. Howard. I thought it would be polite to ask, "How are you, Dr. Howard?" He did not respond immediately and then looked straight at me and said, "Why do you ask?" Fortunately, by this time I had arrived at my floor, and did not have to answer this question.

After Dr. Wilkins's death in 1963, Bob Blizzard and I organized a meeting of the past fellows and their colleagues (a group of over one hundred people). The reunions took place every two years, 1965, 1967, 1969 and 1971. At the last meeting, the Lawson Wilkins Pediatric Endocrine Society was created.

At each of the meetings, a big scientific program was organized. It included a supper with drinks to honor Lawson.

On April 29, 1969, we had our dinner together on the top floor of the School of Hygiene. The food was quite good and we had a great deal of wine that I had bought for the occasion. I had asked Dr. Howard if he would say a few words after dinner. I believe that he was quite touched by my request and he gave the following speech:

> The scientific sessions of the day have passed; we have regaled ourselves with delicious viands and the fruit of the vine. The time has come for more mellow thoughts in our recollection of him in whose memory we are foregathered.
>
> To have been selected to make some remarks on Lawson Wilkins under these circumstances has induced in me rather vigorous emotions, and a consequent fear of inability to do justice to the occasion. For we were close friends as well as enjoying the relationship of coworkers in a medical vineyard from its earliest days of respectability and even before it was respectable. I refer, of course, to the field of clinical endocrinology. Furthermore, there

was the doctor-patient relationship; and, in all of these contexts, a love and admiration for the man continued to grow and flower.

I never knew much about Lawson's youth, medical school years or his time spent in the army during World War I, except that he distinguished himself by devotion to duty and was highly thought of by his seniors in the Hopkins Medical Unit—for example, by Dr. J.M.T. Finney and Dr. Walter Baetjer, who always spoke of him to me retrospectively in the most glowing terms.

You did not come tonight to hear rhetoric of what I have heard of Lawson from others; I have rather tried to record my memories of him as I saw and recall our times together, and there were few dull moments. My first noncasual meeting with Lawson took place, as I recall it, under the aegis of Dr. Park, who had kept telling me that I must know and work with this extraordinary man. The youthful doctor's talents had become evident to Dr. Park early, and he still believes one of his very greatest achievements was in this recognition and in the part he was able to play in the fulfillment of Lawson's great career in academic medicine.

On the day of our meeting arranged by Dr. Park to discuss some of the beautiful observations, which had just been made on skeletal effects of thyroid deficiency in very early life, made with meticulous care and documentation while still actively engaged in practice, I recall distinctly being much less impressed by the beauties of the studies than by the vitality of the man. In response to Dr. Park's gentle knock, the rafters fairly reverberated to the booming voice that urged us to come in; and the sound must have been audible in Washington. This characteristic of his was never out of evidence during our long association and made it impossible for me to exchange confidences with him except in a car or a sound-proof room. Lawson's whispered asides, when, for example, he disliked what a speaker might be saying or the manner of its presentation, could at times cause consternation, for his "that fellow is putting out pure hogwash" might be heard all over the room. But I should hasten to add that his comments were rarely uncomplimentary, for an immense generosity toward the failings of others was one of his most endearing qualities.

The very nature of the man exuded friendliness. Dr. Park has remarked about the late Dr. J.M.T. Finney that a stranger shaking his hand could feel at once the warmth that radiated from him. Lawson, too, had this radiating warmth; and one felt instinctively that his desire was to be kind and on your side if it was in any way in the cards for him to do so.

Another outstanding characteristic of Lawson Wilkins was his patent genuineness. You could literally see right through the man; he wore his heart on his sleeve. This, together with expertise, caused almost adoration in the parents of his patients, and no doubt among the patients, too. Prior to giving up his practice, it was his habit to start work at eight o'clock in the morning, not coming home until eight or nine o'clock in the evening, when Mrs. Wilkins invariably had dinner waiting for him. Between the hours of 12:00 a.m. and 2:00 a.m. he worked on the charts of his studies, meticulously designed and beautifully executed, which became the hallmark of his published investigations. The physical endurance of the man was greater than in anyone I have ever known. Dr. Park has told me that he had offered Lawson charge of the Epileptic Clinic at Harriet Lane, which was declined for lack of interest, and the lack of scope of the problem. But when it was proposed that he head the Pediatric Endocrine unit, this post was accepted. Here he was so successful and his work so original that, with Dr. Park's continued prodding, Lawson finally was persuaded to take a full-time appointment provided by Dr. Schwentker; and his practice was sorrowfully abandoned.

Early in our days of collaboration and friendship, it was, I believe, his suggestion that we meet together once a week and see and discuss some sick persons. If anyone wanted to join, so much the better, for—from their questions or remarks—we might pick up some ideas to pursue, which might enlighten us. Hopefully also there might accrue therefrom something, which might assist the very young and groping efforts then extant to study the field of glandular abnormalities. The operators in this field were at that time demeaned by the rest of the profession to the category of outright quacks or mountebanks. And this categorization was indeed not too far from the truth. The Society for the Study of Internal Secretions used to meet at Atlantic City just before the boardwalk might be filled with the distinguished members of the Association of American Physicians, in whose eyes we hopefully wished to appear in the best possible light. We used to take off our badges on leaving the endocrine meetings before taking our boardwalk stroll. There are probably few or none of you in this room who remember those days, as participants at least. Some of the really corny articles of the then Society for the Study of Internal Secretions are gems of science, which might curdle your blood. Small wonder that Fuller Albright, Allan Kenyon, John Browne, Lawson Wilkins and their like removed their badges before being seen by the Thayers, Longcopes and the Parks.

As a patient himself, Dr. Wilkins left much to be desired. On the first occasion when this relationship began between us, Lawson, then in his early forties, was lying on a couch in great agony from an immense flaming red toe. "Do you think this damned thing is the gout? My father had the gout, you know; but don't touch it if you value your life." His annoyance with the effects of colchicine was nearly as great, or greater than that from the pain in the toe, though it cleared his podagrous symptoms magically. This was before the days of uricosuric agents or enzymatic blockers of uric acid formation, and the advice was required to be much more careful of certain liquid and solid materials of which he was dearly fond. It was characteristic of the flamboyance with, which he went through life that he religiously ignored my advice in this regard. It also may indicate something of the inner and hidden strength of the man, for he had only two or three minor recurrences during the subsequent thirty years. On many occasions he seemed to gain surreptitious pleasure by looking directly at me across a table and waving his glass or his fork when proceeding directly contrary to my medical orders.

In Lawson's later illnesses, the pattern of resistant behavior did not change. After his accident out near Frederick in his tiny car, he steadfastly refused to accept what appeared to me an obviously broken neck (fracture of a cervical vertebra) and constantly fretted with the relatively minor interferences with his activities, which were imposed by the traction and, later, Thomas collar. He drove a car again far earlier than deemed wise by his orthopedist; but despite my pleas that another even minor accident at this time might incapacitate him for all time, he did it and, characteristically, got away with it.

The same fierce hatred of disability characterized his reaction to a very serious coronary occlusion. Added to the burden of immobilization, which alone would have sorely tried him, was the fact that at the time he was ardently courting his second wife, without whose powerful aid I suspect we could never have kept him quiet until such time as his infarction had healed. But the robust joie de vivre returned, and Lawson traveled widely abroad and even climbed mountains for several years before his second coronary finally carried him off. This area of necrosis caused by this first occlusion was so massive that the pathologists could not believe he had been able to do all the things he did right up to his final illness.

But by far the greatest of Lawson's monuments (and no tribute of mine can approach its magnificence) is the presence of you men and women at this dinner. Betsy is a monument in herself, and no mean one. But I refer also to you, his students, who, without undue flattery, make up the core of most distinguished pediatric endocrinologists in the world. And you wouldn't be here if one and all of you were not proud to be called "Lawson's boys." Few men have left behind them so distinguished a group of pupils and colleagues, all crucially influenced in your careers and greatly indebted to that extraordinary man.

It is happy for me that you permitted the Howards to join you and present some of my reflections on a long period as friend and colleague of your guide and mentor. And I am also deeply conscious that some of the encomiums that have come my way have been directly due to my privilege of being coworker with Lawson Wilkins and, for that matter, with most of you also.

42

WORK SCHEDULE AND FINANCING OF THE FELLOWS AT THE PEDIATRIC ENDOCRINE CLINIC

Wilkins's fellows had very defined duties. As time went, it was organized that they were spending their first year of fellowship in the clinic. This was a clinic every morning on weekdays, and there were mainly outpatients and a few inpatients. The charts were dictated by the fellows and then checked by the "chief." In that first year, they were encouraged to consider a clinical study, which could bring them to a laboratory study on their second and third year. At all times, everybody attended the "Saturday Clinic," previously described.

There were also weekly reviews of literature, every Wednesday evening. Usually, we would go out for supper at a Chinese restaurant "Me-Jon-Lo," or the "Steak House." Then we would come back for a couple of hours in the library of the Harriet Lane Home.

At the same time, I had been asked to join NIH meetings to organize the postdoctoral grants. The other colleagues and I agreed that the three year Hopkins plan could be adopted.

In 1959, Lawson took charge of our first training grant (2G-335) followed by a long range grant starting in 1960 (2A-5219). These covered the salaries of five postdocs.

In 1951, Dr. Wilkins had applied for an NIH research grant. When the NIH had started after WWII, there were three branches: cancer, cardiovascular and arthritis and metabolic diseases. At that time, the NIH was made of three buildings, one for each of the departments. Wilkins's grant was in the

Arthritis section (AM-00180). The title was "Relation of Endocrine Glands to Growth and Development."

In 1959, Dr. Wilkins suggested that I apply for a renewal (AM-00180-9). It is of interest that my future work was supported by the same grant until I gave it up in 1995 as AM-00180-44.

Obviously, the emphasis of the research changed with time. At first, it was congenital adrenal hyperplasia. Later, it moved to androgens in the blood and to the first studies of "Testosterone Receptors in Complete Androgen Insensitivity." We also were the first ones to have an assay for aldosterone in blood. The fellows were involved in all these studies.

43

A TRIUMPHANT VISIT TO SOUTH AMERICA (NOVEMBER 1957)

Lawson was invited to visit South America. Lucile and Betsy were included. This was arranged by Dr. Salvador de Majo, the first fellow of the Pediatric Endocrine Clinic in 1948. The Wilkins family was welcomed like royalty everywhere starting in Buenos Aires. Martin and Mercedes Cullen along with Cesar and Estela Bergada were hosts. There were many receptions and also several lectures. The trip went on to Cordoba, Argentina, to visit José and Marina Cara. José had been a fellow in 1954.

After Argentina, there was Brazil, followed by Uruguay, Chile and Peru. The visit to Peru was most vivid to Lawson. They went to Lima at the invitation of Dr. Nicanor Carmona. Lawson explained that Lima was a huge city of several million inhabitants. It was part of the Inca Empire. After the Spanish army's victory, Pizarro founded the city in 1530. Lawson reported that the National University of San Marco was one of the oldest in the world.

Then from Lima, the Wilkins family went to Cuzco and Machu Picchu. Lawson had a great pleasure to describe the ascension by car, train and cable car to the old Inca fortress at 2430 meters. The cable car ride was particularly breathtaking. He had to adjust to the high elevation and he had some trouble but managed to visit the Temple of the Sun, which was the birthplace of the Inca "Virgins of the Sun." In the morning, Machu Picchu was in the clouds that dispersed with the sun. I obtained all the details as given by Dr. Wilkins, when he returned to the clinic.

44

GAINESVILLE, FLORIDA (NOVEMBER 1958)

The fellows and staff of the Pediatric Endocrine Clinic had close contacts with the people of the Adult Endocrine Clinic. This was in part due to the fact that the pediatricians attended the weekly clinic of John Eager Howard in Hurd Hall, and the adult fellows attended the Saturday clinics of Lawson Wilkins. Two of the adult group were William Thomas and Tom Connor.

Eventually Bill Thomas left Hopkins for a position as the Chief Endocrinologist at the Medical School of Gainesville, which had just opened. Bill asked me to come and give a lecture, which was fun. However, it also brought up the possibility that I could move to Florida. The school was brand new and attractive, and the dean was pleasant. I would become Associate Professor and would be given a large lab for which I would ask what were my specific requirements for research. This offer was attractive.

I suspect that Dr. William Thomas must have written to Lawson Wilkins about me. I was given a copy of the answer:

Dear Bill,

As you well know, I cannot speak too highly of Claude Migeon from both his personal and scientific qualifications for the position, which you are offering him. He has a thorough grasp of the fundamental problems of steroid chemistry and real scientific ability in investigating them. He shows great clarity of thought and his papers are examples of accurate, scientific writing. He has a good grasp of all the problems of endocrinology. His work has been a great aid diagnostically on both the pediatric and the adult endocrine side here. As you know, his own interests go deeper into basic problems of steroid metabolism, the binding of steroids in plasma and their transmission across the placenta.

If Claude should leave here, our work in pediatric endocrinology and our training of men in this field would be insuperably handicapped. I trust that every effort will be made to keep him here. I am expecting to retire from the administrative responsibilities of the pediatric endocrinological division next July, although I may have to continue responsibility under my present research grant until July 1960 and expected to continue my connections on the clinical side for another five years. I think, therefore, that the planning and offers for Claude Migeon will depend largely upon Dr. Cooke and whomever is to be selected for my position. I sincerely hope that you will not press Claude too rapidly for a decision but will give him an opportunity to learn what plans are being formulated here.

With my best personal regards.

Yours sincerely,
Lawson Wilkins

Lawson asked me if I had read his letter and wanted to know what I needed to keep me happy. I suggested a promotion and increase in salary. My salary was very low and when I asked for a raise from Dr. Robert Cooke, he said that I was a bachelor with little needs.

However, when I realized that Lawson thought that he needed me, I said that I would stay at Hopkins, and I told so to Bill Thomas. Eventually my promotion came, and later I obtained an NIH grant of Clinical Research Scientists. Dr. Cooke also gave me a check of $10,000 to go study the transplacental passage of steroids during pregnancy in Stockholm at the Karolinksa Hospital with Dr. Carl Gemzell, chief of obstetrics.

45

BETSY WILKINS'S WEDDING (DECEMBER 1958)

Lawson was strongly in favor of marriage. He would bring up the idea of marriage very indirectly, reporting how much Lucile was a wonderful support for him. He would mention how he could always share the troubles of his life with her and would recall how much fun she was.

In early spring of 1958, I visited Seymour Lieberman at the Presbyterian Hospital in New York City. After the visit, I met with Betsy Wilkins who was working at New York Hospital. I felt that I should be kind to Betsy, not only because she was the daughter of Lawson but also because I was much older than she was.

Lawson told me that Betsy had met Philip McMaster in New York, a young man who had graduated from Hopkins and was an intern at New York Hospital. Later, he joined the NIH Department of Immunology. Phil's father was a well-known scientist at Rockefeller Institute in New York City, who deeply impressed Lawson.

Lawson and Lucile were also impressed with their future son-in-law. As a romantic woman, Lucile was looking forward to a June wedding. However, Betsy and Philip decided to get married earlier.

The preparations took place actively and the wedding took place in December of 1958. This was a great celebration. Lawson had his high hat, Lucile wore a magnificent dress and Betsy had a splendid white wedding dress. Unfortunately, I had to get secondhand information about the wedding and marriage, as I was in Chicago for the end of year celebrations with the Nanos family.

46

LUCILE'S DEATH
(JUNE 10, 1959)

The first week in May 1959, Lucile had a seizure. It was not clear what this was related to. Dr. Wilkins, after a few days, took his wife to Johns Hopkins. He was very concerned and did not communicate much.

Because of the personal love of Dr. Judson Van Wyk for the Wilkins family, I wanted to give him the news. Here is my letter:

Dear Jud,

I thought you would be interested to hear about the health of Mrs. Wilkins. Dr. Wilkins is so concerned about it that he has stopped coming to his office and does not take telephone calls and spends all his time with his wife.

As you probably know, the trouble started in Atlantic City when Mrs. Wilkins had a mild seizure, which followed a short period of difficulty so far as sense of equilibrium and coordination. For this reason Dr. Wilkins did not go to the pediatric meetings at Buck Hill Falls and brought Mrs. Wilkins back to Baltimore to be hospitalized in Marburg where she was checked by a group of neurologists and neurosurgeons. At first it was thought that a subdural hematoma was at the origin of her trouble. An arteriogram, however, did not demonstrate any such hematoma. On Thursday, May 14, a scanogram revealed the existence of a brain tumor, which was thought to be located near very vital centers such as speech and coordination centers (I am not a great neurologists, I am just telling you what information I obtained from Dave Clark). That same day Dr. Wilkins and the neurologists had a meeting to decide on the possibility of an exploration. This was a most difficult situation for Dr. Wilkins. Eventually, he asked Dr. Park's advice and it was decided to do a pneumoencephalogram followed by an exploration. These two procedures were carried out this morning. The neurosurgeon, Dr. Chambers, found a rather wild sort of tumor, which he could not remove. A biopsy was performed and this is the present situation.

I don't have to tell you how much Dr. Wilkins is upset. I wish there were something we could do to help him, but it seems that he would rather be left alone, at least at the present time. I will keep you informed of any further development.

As ever,
Claude

Following my letter, a few weeks passed by during which Lucile had gone back home. Dr. Wilkins had passed the word for us not to interfere. Of course, we did not.

However, the symptoms were becoming more intense and the seizures more frequent.

I think a decision had been made to attempt an ablation of the tumor, in view of its present progression. So, Mrs. Wilkins came back to the third floor of the Marburg Building and she was scheduled for surgery.

One evening, I was working late in the lab. I decided to go to the Marburg Building to visit Mrs. Wilkins at about 9:00 p.m. I managed to find her room. She was alone, awake. She was pleased to see me and to talk. She explained that it was strange; she was trying to pour tea without knowing whether or not she was pouring into a cup. We both decided that it was sad, but funny, and we laughed.

I tried not to get Lucile tired and I excused myself. Then she told me that her surgery was the next morning. I assured her that everything would be OK, even if I did not believe so. We said good-bye and I gave her a kiss. Then she said, "Claude, I am scared." I patted her head and left, unable to speak as tears came to my eyes.

I believe she never recovered from surgery and on June 10, 1959, she passed away. The funeral was held at the Episcopal Church of the Redeemer, where Betsy and Phil were married less than six months earlier. It was very sad and I cried.

47

BARBARA RUBEN MIGEON, MD AND DR. LAWSON WILKINS (1959-1960)

Barbara had come to the House staff of the Department of Pediatrics at Hopkins in 1956. We dated for three years before a marriage decision was made. Between her interest in Pediatric Endocrinology and our dating, Barbara had contacts with Lawson Wilkins. For this reason, I have asked her to report her impressions and memories. So here are Barbara's writings:

I met Lawson Wilkins shortly after arriving at Hopkins as a Pediatric Intern in 1956. He had served as director of the Department of Pediatrics for the two previous years. Although he had already gleefully relinquished that job to Bob Cooke, he continued to give a Christmas party for faculty of the department, housestaff, as well as his endocrine fellows. It was a warm lovely occasion, with music and singing. I caught my first glimpse of Claude Migeon that night, admiring him as he sang "Chevaliers de la table rounde, dites moi si le vin est bon" with Victor Najjar at the piano. As a house officer, I remember Lawson's making rounds with us, never bothered if there wasn't a proper endocrine patient in the house. He would go up to the bed of some obese child and discuss why that child was not hypothyroid. As soon as I could, during my second year in the pediatric residency program, I elected a rotation in the endocrine clinic. I spent almost four months there.

Part of Lawson's gift as a teacher was his ability to make his pupils feel smart. He managed to make me think that I, a young resident, could teach *him* something. Highly appreciative of any initiative, he made me feel very clever to have diagnosed a child with the hypertensive form of congenital adrenal hyperplasia, because I had accurately measured the infant's blood pressure. I especially enjoyed his Saturday morning clinic held in the Harriet Lane Outpatient Department. I remember how he always narrated each patient's entire clinical history, starting from the very beginning, so that any clinician coming in for the first time—even a novice—could understand the significant findings, and concluding with the present visit. Fortunately for me, one of his postdoctoral fellows was unable to carry out his responsibilities, and so I acted as a substitute fellow for several months. During that time, I learned from example how to meticulously care for patients and to learn from them at the same time. Because the experience was so satisfying, I proposed him the possibility of postponing my last year of residency and staying on as his fellow, at least until the end of the year. However, even though he needed help, Lawson discouraged that idea, insisting that I finish the residency program.

By the end of my Pediatric House staff training, I was certain that I wanted to become an endocrinologist. I asked Lawson for a job, trying to convince him that it would be wise to take me as a postdoctoral fellow. But, he was equally certain that women should not be examining male genitalia. Having never had a female fellow, he encouraged me to get my training elsewhere. He seemed a bit uncomfortable telling me of his lack of enthusiasm for my being one of "the boys" (as he called his fellows). However, as he was not averse to having me in his clinic in another capacity, he suggested that I work in the lab with Claude. He was unaware at that time that Claude and I had an extramural relationship, which eliminated that possibility. As an alternative to staying at Hopkins, he suggested that I apply for a position with his former fellow, John Crigler, who was the chief of the division of endocrinology at Children's Hospital in Boston. He also encouraged me to apply for an individual postdoctoral fellowship from NIH. Both applications were supported by generous letters of recommendation (he gave me copies of his letters). I received my fellowship and the position in Boston.

That might have been the end of our relationship, except for the fact that after only a year in Boston, I returned to Baltimore and Hopkins to continue my postdoctoral training in genetics with Barton Childs...and to marry Claude.

Figure 29a. Barbara Migeon in Paris on the Pont des Arts

48

MARRIAGE OF BARBARA AND CLAUDE MIGEON WITH DR. WILKINS (APRIL 1960)

I dated Barbara for about three years. She was working with the Pediatric Endocrine Group. The fellows were William Cleveland and Robert Stempfel in 1959 to 1960. They both admired Barbara and advised me to marry her.

Barbara joined us at the Consultation, the Journal Club on Wednesday night when we went to dinner at the Chinese restaurant Me-Jon-Lo, or at the Steak House.

I guess that I was slow making the decision of marrying despite the advice of William and Bob. So, on July 1959, Barbara moved to Boston.

The separation brought back the decision to get married. Barbara was for eloping, as her family was concerned about our union.

So, Barbara invited William Cleveland and his wife Marty to be our witnesses. Because a civil marriage could not take place in Baltimore at that time, we made arrangements with a Justice of the Peace in Alexandria, Virginia.

Barbara flew from Boston on a Thursday night. On Friday, we went to buy our rings. We made plans to drive to Alexandria with William and Marty Cleveland. However, there was an extra guest as described below by Barbara:

> Claude had always considered Lawson somewhat like a father, so he felt obliged to tell him that we were planning to elope. Lawson said, "Good, when do we go?" and he did come along for the trip to the justice of the peace in Arlington, Virginia. Along with Bill and Marty Cleveland we arrived one Saturday after sundown on April 2, 1960. The JP was an old man with Parkinson's disease, and pinned to his lapel was the French Croix de Guerre. Our

wedding vows were delayed for at least ten minutes while Lawson and his new friend discussed their adventures in France during the First World War. The wedding was followed by an elegant supper at Chez François, a well-known French restaurant in Washington, DC, where Lawson announced he was buying the drinks, and needless to say we had a merry time. Driving back to Baltimore very late that night, the five of us were in the midst of an animated discussion of several endocrine patients, when Lawson abruptly stopped the conversation, saying in his booming voice, "Well I'll be damned! This is the first time I have discussed male pseudohermaphroditism with a bride at her wedding." The following year, we were able to reciprocate by accompanying him to a courthouse in Washington where he married Teence Anderson.

49

HONEYMOON IN SCOTLAND, COPENHAGEN AND PARIS

Written by Barbara:

Not only was he a part of our tiny wedding party, but he went along on our honeymoon. As our excuse to spend several weeks in Europe, Claude and I were taking advantage of two endocrine meetings held back to back in July 1960. One was the meeting about the adrenal gland at the Royal Scottish Automobile Club in Glasgow, and the other, The First International Congress of Endocrinology in Copenhagen. For the weekend between the two meetings, we had made plans to visit Dr. James Farquar, a pediatric endocrinologist at his home in Edinburgh. Lawson rented a car, and we took a very scenic route, stopping at Loch Lomond in a fine "Scotch mist," and on to Stirling Castle, where Dr. Wilkins regaled us with stories of the bloody deeds that had occurred there centuries before; he gleefully showed us the blood spots on the floor, which he accurately attributed to a murder committed there by King James the Second. He fondly recalled having previously visited this bloody spot with Lucile. Always an astute observer, he pointed out the bales of hay in the Scottish fields, telling us that if he was parachuted into any country he would know where he was by the way the hay was packaged.

At the end of this delightful day, we arrived at the Farquars, and were warmly greeted by them. However, although it was the cocktail hour, no alcohol was offered, because as we soon realized, our lovely hostess, Mary Farquar, was a teetotaler. Lawson hinted that a drink might be welcome, telling our host, "In Maryland, we drink rye, but the scotch should be very good in Scotland." However, none was forthcoming. At the end of the weekend, after lunch with the Farquars at the country home of the Regius Professor of Pediatrics, Richard Ellis, in the shadow of the ruins of Crookston Castle, (where Lord Darnley honeymooned with Mary Queen of Scots) we were driving through the beautiful Tweed River Valley. Stopping momentarily to enjoy the view, we returned to the car, but found that it was unwilling to move one step further—perhaps in rebellion because Lawson was not a gentle driver. When the mechanics arrived to take the car to a garage and us into Peebles, the nearest town, the car started for them without difficulty. While waiting for the chauffeur to take us back to Glasgow Airport, we decided to have dinner and a glass of that elusive scotch at the only hotel in town. However, it was seven o'clock on Sunday, and the kitchen was closed and because of blue-laws there was no drink to be had. Lawson and Claude headed for a nearby pub, where they charmed the pub keeper. Although impossible to get a glass of scotch, she suggested that, as travelers, they could buy the whole bottle. Meanwhile, I had managed to find some cheddar cheese and crackers. In the lobby of the hotel, we devoured the cheese and finished off the bottle by the time our car arrived. The chauffeur told us he hadn't slept in three days, so Lawson kept up a continuous conversation to keep him awake during the journey to the airport.

In Copenhagen, Lawson saw patients as a consultant to Henning Andersen, the Danish pediatric endocrinologist. Henning considered himself a Wilkins fellow as he had spent several months at Hopkins. Enriched by his well-earned and unexpected consultation fee, Lawson invited us to join him and the Andersens for supper at Oscar Davison's, a restaurant renowned for its lobster and *Aquavit*, which were both replenished whenever the plate or glass was emptied. The time spent together that summer was a memorable, intoxicating, and a bonding experience for us.

Then, we went to France. Barbara was introduced to the Migeon family for the first time. She had problems with language as my family did not speak English. But she managed very well.

After five weeks away, we were ready to return to Baltimore. But before we had left, we had looked at houses with Lawson. One of them in Homeland was nice and we gave a bid slightly lower than the asking price. It was not accepted. At that point, we gave my family's address in France as the contact address, if they wanted to change their minds.

And they did. So, in Rethel at my parents' house, we found that we were the proud owners of a house. We had forgotten the details of the house and were anxious to face the facts and our new habitation.

50

RETURN TO BALTIMORE (JUNE 1960)

O ur first move once in Baltimore was to go see our new house. We had forgotten some of the details of our home, after our honeymoon in Europe
with Dr. Wilkins.

Barbara Migeon described our return as follows:

> In Baltimore, Lawson had been deeply involved in our search for a
> house, and in resodding the lawn of the one we purchased. To our
> surprise we awoke one morning to find that our front yard was
> piled high with several tons of dirt and sod, which he had ordered
> for us. The following Sunday, all day, Lawson, Claude and John
> Eckert, an endocrine fellow, distributed the soil around the house,
> and sowed grass seed. Shortly thereafter, while Lawson was out
> of town, as a visiting lecturer, we received a telegram from him. It
> said, "Lovely weather for growing grass. Keep it wet."

When we were in Copenhagen, we had bought several pieces of furniture made
of teak wood at Illums Bolighus, a great department store. Lawson had insisted
on paying for a lovely tea table. After he had seen our chimney, he decided that we
needed to have fireplace equipment. He bought all the necessary pieces, including a
metal mantle that isolated the fireplace from the room, and he installed everything.

Because he was quite lonely, he came often for supper in our kitchen, particularly during weekends. He loved everything we cooked and appreciated a good
wine with the meal. On September 21, 1960, we had dinner with the parents of
Barbara. Her father, a family medicine doctor for many years, got along amazingly well with Lawson. They had the same feelings about the practice of medicine.

51

LAWSON WILKINS'S FIRST CORONARY (OCTOBER 1960)

Following Lucile's death, Lawson was rather despondent. So, he spent a lot of time with us. He invited himself to our wedding, and our honeymoon in Glasgow, Edinburgh, the Tweed River Country in Scotland, the Loch Ness and Copenhagen.

After, Barbara and I settled in our new house, Dr. Wilkins was often a guest. He attended the visit of the Bergada family from Buenos Aires, Argentina. He also was with us when the mother of one of his patients, the Marquisse di Fontiere from Lisbon, Portugal, visited our home with her son. There was also the visit of the Ambassador of Yugoslavia, Mr. Nikesic, as his sister Maria was a fellow in our clinic.

In addition, Lawson was often our "kitchen company" on Sunday nights, when we had a simple meal together. When he did not arrive on time one Sunday, we were concerned. Then, he phoned from Hopkins, in a private patient room at Marburg Building saying, "I won't be there for supper, I had a coronary." He told us not to worry and that he wouldn't die. "I have met a wonderful woman, and I want to live. If I had not met that woman, I would have run up and down the steps of my house to finish my life, but now, I want to live."

We thought that the old man was delirious, so we went to Hopkins and found him with an IV and an oxygen line and his pack of cigarettes on the nightstand. He repeated what he had said on the phone. I told him I was going to call Betsy and Phil in Paris. He insisted that if I told them, I would say they did not have to come home because it was a mild incident and that he was very well taken care of.

The next morning before work, I went to see him; he appeared to be in good shape. He told me to come back ten minutes before 5:00 p.m., because he needed me as a chaperone, when his wonderful lady friend would come to visit.

Of course, I came at the right time, just before a very nice, smiling lady arrived at his room. Lawson introduced me from his bed to Mrs. Catrina Anderson Francis. After some thirty minutes of simple conversation about health and how Lawson was doing, they talked about boats on the Chesapeake Bay. After a while, the nice lady excused herself and went away.

After she had left, Lawson wanted to know what I thought of her. It was clear that he expected me to say that Mrs. Anderson was wonderful. Lawson told me further that he was looking forward to leaving the hospital so he could propose to her. He asked if I would help him by chaperoning his meeting with "Teence," her nickname. His joy was palpable, contagious, but was it unrealistic?

During his stay at Hopkins, John Eager Howard took care of him. Lawson did not like the hospital life, the nurses, the medications or the requirement to rest in bed. Dr. Raphael David, his fellow, spent a great deal of time with Lawson. There were many visitors including Teence.

52

DISCHARGE HOME (NOVEMBER 1960)

Eventually, Wilkins was sent home to rest for a month. As Betsy was in Paris, Barbara and I moved in with him. It was very difficult to deal with Lawson who always wanted to do more than he was supposed to.

To make the situation more complicated, I had a meeting planned in France. I had to leave Barbara in charge with the help of a nurse. Here is a report from Barbara from that time:

> Dr. Wilkins asked us to chaperone Teence's visits at the hospital and at home. As his daughter, Betsy, was living abroad at the time, and because we thought he might need companionship during his post-hospital recovery period, Claude and I moved in with him for the first two weeks after he returned to his home. I was there when John Eager Howard came to tell Lawson that he had won the prestigious Koch Medal from the American Endocrine Society. Dr. Howard asked that I leave the room, while he told him. I had no idea what the secret was, but I was sure that I would know all about it after Dr. Howard left. And I did, as Lawson was pleased by the news, and not good at keeping any kind of secret.

During their close living together, Barbara had time to discuss many things with Lawson. This was the time when Barbara was becoming a geneticist. Here are her remarks:

> Quick to appreciate any novel treatment or other innovation that could facilitate the care of his patients or investigation of their

disease, Wilkins was eager to have it for his patients. Shortly, after my return to Hopkins, I became one of those carrying out the analysis of human chromosomes soon after it was possible to do so, at first in the Cytogenetics Laboratory in the Moore clinic, which was directed by visiting professor Malcolm Ferguson Smith, and then in my own laboratory in the Department of Pediatrics. I recently reread one of the many notes I received from Lawson asking me to see that chromosome studies were carried out on a variety of his patients, which he suspected might have a chromosomal abnormality. Included were the females with Turner syndrome that he called "his synthetic brides," proud that he could make them almost perfect females by treating them with estrogen. He had long before looked for the presence of a sex chromatin body, or Barr body in his patients, and had classified them as sex chromatin positive or sex chromatin negative. However at that time, the origin of the Barr body was not understood, so that chromosome analysis would be more informative. He was among the first to identify the nature of sex chromosomes in the true hermaphrodites and in his patients with non-classic Turner syndrome. As he suspected because they had a sex chromatin body, they were not forty-five X but had forty-six chromosomes with a second X chromosome, which most often was abnormal. And how excited he was to learn the results of these studies!

As you can see, despite his having deprived me of the pleasure of being one of his "boys," Lawson had an influential role in my academic career, and we were very fond of one another. But early in our relationship, after a couple of drinks, he might say. "I love you and Ralph David (one of his "boys" who was an Egyptian Jew), but I don't care much for Jewish people." Once he told me that the German Jews in Baltimore, the department store merchants like the Hutzlers and Hochschilds, were fine people, but that the second wave of Jewish immigrants, the Russian Jews, destroyed his neighborhood (his family's home was on Broadway). I answered, "but *I* am a Russian Jew," and the subject never came up again. Clearly he felt uncomfortable about this bias, as he brought it up from time to time, almost apologetically. I have no doubt that it arose from his recollections of his childhood. However, it was only talk, as he never treated anyone with anything but respect, and one's race or ethnic group never influenced the quality of care, or how he dealt with colleagues, students, and patients. Unlike the situation in other clinics, he did not distinguish between private and non-paying patients; they all got the same meticulous care and respectful treatment. I remember Lawson fondly as a gifted raconteur, extraordinary teacher, and outstanding clinical investigator. Especially memorable were his strong intellectual curiosity, his sense of history, his intense interest in all he surveyed, and his being my good friend.

53

LAWSON AND TEENCE'S WEDDING (APRIL 1961)

D r. Wilkins was a gregarious man who needed company at all times. When he lost Lucile in 1959, he was very lonely. He spent a lot of time with Barbara and me, including our wedding, honeymoon, his cardiac accident and recovery.

It also included his relationship with Teence and his marriage with her. Actually, we were pleased that he had found companionship with Teence, a divorcée of about sixty years of age. Her brother, Mr. Anderson, was a lawyer and friend of Lawson.

One day, Dr. Wilkins came into my small office on the fifth floor of Harriet Lane Home. He settled himself on the only chair available and started to tell me about his decision of getting married again. It was going to be a civil marriage in Washington, DC, with the details supervised by Mr. Anderson. A court judge of DC would officiate.

Lawson asked that Barbara and I attend the ceremony. He gave me the time and place it would take place. We would all drive together from Baltimore. We were to leave several hours before the time, as we could not be late. He wanted me to drive slowly behind his car, so in case his car had a problem, we could drive them to Washington on time.

Thirty minutes before the hour agreed to meet, Dr. Wilkins arrived at our home on Thornhill Road. Barbara and I jumped into our car and the procession of Lawson first and we closely behind took off for Washington. We arrived safely, early enough to have time to meet with a few relatives of Teence, including her son of one of her two previous marriages.

The official ceremony was quite simple and short. At the end, we all embraced. Lawson was the happiest I had ever seen him.

Betsy could not attend the ceremony, because she was in Paris with Phil, who had a two-year fellowship in Immunochemistry at the Pasteur Institute. As for Barbara and me, we had to return to Baltimore promptly.

54

THE HONEYMOON OF LAWSON AND TEENCE WILKINS (OCTOBER 1961)

After the marriage in Washington, DC, Lawson and Teence came back to their Edgevale Road home. Barbara, Jacques, our one-month-old son and I were invited one Sunday to their home. Also invited was a fellow, Dr. Paul Malvaux, his wife and baby son. The Malvaux came from Leuven in Flanders in Belgium. Paul worked at the Université de Louvain. During lunch, the Wilkins talked about their plans for their honeymoon, asking us for advice.

Their first stop would be in Paris where they would meet with Betsy and Phil. Then there was the possibility of going to Provence in France and Rome in Italy. Lawson definitely wanted to go to Egypt to see the Pyramids and Sphinx in Cairo.

After lunch, we wished them a good trip and left. I heard about the trip after their return. Lawson was happy to see Betsy and Phil in Paris. They stayed several days and had a great time exploring the city with them. They also went to visit Ireland. (Figure 30)

Next, I heard a lot about the Pyramids and the Sphinx with its broken nose from a cannon shot from Napoleon I. Teence had ridden on the back of a camel, while Lawson refused to do so, thinking it was not dignified for him. I told Dr. Wilkins that this reminded me of an experience I had had when we went to a very small island, Hydra, in the Cyclades, south of Athens. This island had no cars. When Barbara and I disembarked from our boat, the hotel had sent several donkeys to pick us up. First, the man put our luggage on the first donkey. Then he picked up Barbara and put her on the back of the second donkey before she could say anything. When he came to grab me, I refused very loudly, and the man did not resist. We started our walk toward the hotel. When one of the donkeys had droppings, the caravan stopped, the man collected the stuff very carefully and deposited it in bags, which were on the back of a fourth donkey. At the end of my story, Dr. Wilkins had a good laugh and he understood that I did not think that it was dignified to ride a donkey, either. At the same time, Lawson reminded me that Jesus had ridden a donkey in the Bible.

Figure 30. Lawson and Teence during their
honeymoon voyage in Ireland. (1961)

55

DEATH OF LAWSON
(SEPTEMBER 27, 1963)

Early in the morning of September 27, I got a phone call from Teence Wilkins. She asked me if I could come to Edgevale Road because Lawson felt much worse and could not move from bed. I said I would come immediately. I drove there and saw another car already parked in front of the house. I ran up the steps from the street to the house and rang the doorbell. Teence opened the door and told me that Dr. John Eager Howard was there and she took me upstairs to Lawson's bedroom.

There, I found John Eager Howard auscultating Lawson who had great difficulty breathing. My "Good morning, Dr. Wilkins" did not get a response. When John Eager Howard was finished, he turned to me and gave me a syringe and a couple of test tubes. He requested that I draw Lawson's blood and carry it to the lab at Hopkins.

John Eager Howard and I were very concerned to see the chief in such a low status. Dr. Wilkins could not respond to me. I had to get his arm, put it in position and I took the blood without any trouble.

I told Dr. Wilkins that I hoped he was going to feel better soon. Then I left for Hopkins Hospital and delivered the blood with the prescription of John Eager Howard. Afterwards, I went to the third floor of the Children's Medical and Surgical Center and told Bob Blizzard and my other colleagues, as well as the secretaries and technicians that Dr. Wilkins was gravely ill. We were all greatly concerned.

A few hours later, I got another phone call from Teence. She told me that Lawson had been transported to Hopkins to be hospitalized. I went to Osler 4 rapidly. I met with Dr. Richard Ross, the cardiologist, in the corridor and asked about Lawson. His statement was very terse: "Dr. Wilkins is in complete cardiac failure."

I went to his room. It was a sad spectacle. The chief was as pale as his sheets, lying down with oxygen therapy and a gastric tube. He was unable to speak. He saw me and made a motion asking for a piece of paper and pencil. After I asked how he felt, he wrote, "Claude, I am very tired." I tried to say something appropriate, but I admit that I did not know what to say. I ended up saying, "You are going to feel better, Dr. Wilkins." He looked at me, shook his head and closed his eyes, clearly in pain. At that point, the nurse ushered me out of the room. That was the last I saw of Lawson Wilkins.

I went home to Barbara and my two little boys, Jacques and Jean-Paul. I could have cried at the sight of the contrast between near-death at the hospital and new life in our home.

The next morning, Teence called me and reported that Lawson had passed away peacefully in the night. Betsy McMaster had seen her dad before he died. Teence asked me to let the past fellows know as soon as possible. I went to Hopkins and personally called Alfred Bongiovanni, Jud Van Wyk, George Clayton, Melvin Grumbach and William Cleveland. The secretaries had a list of numbers and made calls to many fellows and colleagues of Lawson as well.

It was very difficult for me to focus on what to do. I went to the Wilkins' home, where there was a lot going on and I felt like an outsider. I returned to Hopkins for a while and then went home where I had to help with our two-year-old, Jacques, and two-week-old, Jean-Paul.

Eventually, Teence and Betsy let me know that the funeral would be at the Episcopal Church of the Redeemer on Charles Street. Barbara could not attend because of the new baby. I went by myself and met a number of the past fellows.

During the service, I could not stop tears from rolling down my face. I tried concentrating on the stained glass windows on the right side of the chapel, but this did little to prevent the tears.

Teence arranged to have the past fellows who were present to carry the casket of the chief. I tried to hide my sadness, unsuccessfully. We were directed toward a car to carry the casket to the cemetery. And this was the end.

On October 5, 1963, I received a kind note from Betsy McMaster:

Dear Claude,

I cannot begin to tell you how much it has meant to all of us to have your help and companionship throughout the past few days. You had such a special place among "Daddy's boys" and we appreciate beyond all words all you have done for him over the years.

Sincerely,
Betsy

It is quite ironic that our son, Jean-Paul, was born on September 12, 1963 and Lawson had visited mother and child in their room at Hopkins. Dr. Wilkins died two weeks later, September 27. Five weeks later, his grandson, Charles, was born.

Eventually, I went back to work at the Pediatric Endocrine Clinic, which had just moved from Harriet Lane to the third floor of the Children's Medical and Surgical Center (CMSC-3). I joined Bob Blizzard, the fellows and the technicians, keeping memories of Dr. Lawson Wilkins.

56

THE LEGACY OF LAWSON WILKINS: A NEW MEDICAL SPECIALTY, PEDIATRIC ENDOCRINOLOGY

At this point, it is important to outline the contributions of Dr. Wilkins to the medical field. He is often referred to as the "Father of Pediatric Endocrinology." Indeed, he came to the field of Pediatrics at a time when it was subdivided into specialties. He and his textbook *The Diagnosis and Treatment of Endocrine Disorders in Childhood and Adolescence* (First Edition, 1950) were the basis of this new field.

How he came to this is well presented by one of his early fellows, Judson J. Van Wyk who gave a conference on the subject in October 28, 2003, and is reported here as follows:

Tale of Lawson Wilkins
By Judson Van Wyk
October 28, 2003

Many were surprised to learn that Dr. Wilkins was a general pediatrician in private practice until he was over fifty. Wilkins's father was a general practitioner in Baltimore whose hero was William Osler. Lawson sometimes drove the horse and buggy for his father on his rounds and later cited his dad as one of the three most important influences on his career, the others being Fuller Albright and Edwards Park.

Lawson attended Johns Hopkins Medical School, but received his MD in France, where he had spent his fourth year as an orderly on the battlefields of World War I. On his return he took a medical internship at Yale and a pediatric residency in Pediatrics at the Harriet Lane Home under John Howland.

Wilkins's solo practice as a private pediatrician in Baltimore gave him the freedom to spend part of each week in one of the specialty clinics: such as the syphilis clinic or the epilepsy clinic. His first paper in 1923 was on the potassium content of human serum, carried out by a laborious gravimetric assay method.

(He was also interested in calcium metabolism and rickets. He wrote a few early papers in collaboration with Drs. Orr W.J., Holt L.E., Jr, Boone FH and Kramer, B.)

In 1935, Dr. Edwards Park, chief of Pediatrics at the Harriet Lane Home had the wisdom to foresee that the new discipline of Endocrinology might be of value in understanding the growth and development of children; he showed even greater wisdom by asking Wilkins to organize a pediatric endocrine clinic. Wilkins resisted: "Do you want to make a charlatan out of me?"

Nevertheless Wilkins accepted the challenge and spent every evening into the small hours reading the fat tomes written by so-called "experts" in the field. Wilkins became increasingly frustrated by the absence of any science and the long convoluted descriptions of endless "glandular syndromes." Lawson was never one to suffer fools gladly, and his most important act one night while reading in bed was to fling the volume against the wall while cursing the stuffed shirts who could write such garbage.

He decided to begin over from scratch and learn everything he could by carefully documenting every clinical feature of his patients, and exploiting every opportunity to learn about mechanisms. Wilkins had little knowledge of statistics, but had a penetrating eye for what each of his patients could teach him. He had long ago adopted the practice of plotting all of his patients' findings graphically as a function of time in the hope that such graphs might provide correlations and insights that might otherwise be missed.

Lacking centile growth charts as we now know them, Lawson adopted the 1932 charts of Engelbach, which gave average values for age of height, weight, span, segmental proportions, and circumferences of the head, chest, and abdomen. He adopted these charts because they permitted correlations of body proportions with growth parameters.

He also laboriously traced out the appearance of epiphyses in the wrist, elbow, shoulder, knee, and ankle and developed his own scheme for determining bone age long before Greulich's Atlas based on wrist X-rays.

Hypothyroidism

He started by studying hypothyroidism, plotting the effect of thyroid substitution treatment and its withdrawal on parameters of growth and development. His 1938 paper(I) was his first contribution of the effect of an endocrine deficiency on growth. In it, he charted chronologic age versus the different measures of developmental age. He concluded from his many such graphs that bone maturation was the most sensitive indicator of adequate substitution therapy.

Wilkins recognized, however, that to understand the physiological effects of thyroid and other hormones, he had to turn to the laboratory, a task for which he was ill-prepared. But he was a good judge of talent and had the good fortune to meet Walter Fleischmann, a refugee Viennese physiologist. When the *Journal of Clinical Endocrinology* made its debut in 1941, the first two papers in each of the first two issues were by Wilkins and Fleischmann reporting their studies in hypothyroidism.(8-II)

Since there were no methods available to measure thyroid hormone levels directly, he measured the effects of thyroid on lowering the elevated cholesterol in hypothyroid children and raising the depressed levels of creatine in the urine. He found these measures far more reliable than measurements of basal metabolic rate.

It should come as no surprise, therefore, to learn that Wilkins had one of the first binary counters in Baltimore to study thyroid problems with radioactive iodine uptake studies, and one of the first to order the new protein bound iodine measurements on his patients.

In 1944, Wilkins went through a period of despondency following the tragic death of his only son. He was rescued by Dr. Park, who induced him to become a full-time member of the Johns Hopkins Department of Pediatrics.

Wilkins brought with him his vast collection of case histories and photographs. He presented this extensive collection in a gigantic poster at the First International Congress of Pediatrics in Zurich in 1950.

He then collated this material into the first *Textbook of Pediatric Endocrinology*. This launched, his fame spread rapidly, and students from the US and many foreign countries flocked to study under him. His textbook was considered the "Bible" of the field at the time.

Congenital Adrenal Hyperplasia

Wilkins was particularly challenged by difficulties encountered by patients with congenital adrenal hyperplasia. He knew that the secretions of adrenal androgens were controlled by ACTH and he made several unsuccessful attempts to suppress ACTH secretion by administering biologically weak androgens. When cortisone became available for experimental use, Wilkins immediately saw it as a more likely participant in the ACTH feedback mechanism, and in short order was able to show that the secretion of adrenal androgens in girls with CAH could be inhibited by the administration of a glucocorticoid hormone.(52, 58) Bartter and Albright in Boston made the same observation independently. Crigler and other postdoctoral fellows followed these initial reports with a series of classic studies that provided the essential data for long term adrenal suppression of these patients.(60-63)

Wilkins thought that the identification of steroid precursors in the urine of patients with CAH might reveal to us the biosynthetic pathways of human adrenal steroid biogenesis. Most steroid biochemists, however, were preoccupied with perfusing bovine adrenals with radio-labeled precursors and could not be bothered by clinical problems. Eventually he enlisted Dr. Seymour Lieberman in this endeavor and Lieberman accepted Wilkins's prospective research associate, Dr. Alfred Bongiovanni, into his laboratory to learn advanced steroid methodology. As Wilkins had predicted, the studies of Bongiovanni led to the definition of the crucial enzymatic lesions in the different forms of adrenal hyperplasia.(75)

Al pioneered the pregnantriol method for monitoring adrenal suppression, and contributed greatly to our knowledge of the enzymatic defects in the several forms of CAH. Al and Walter Eberlein described and identified the defect in 11β-hydroxylase deficiency.

Syndrome of Gonadal Dysgenesis and Sex Differentiation

Another early interest of Wilkins was sexual development. He was particularly intrigued by the syndrome of short stature, sexual infantilism, and multiple congenital anomalies in girls. This syndrome was not uncommon, and Henry Turner's description had previously been described by a number of other authors. In 1942, two groups, Varney, Kenyon, and Koch in Chicago and Albright and his coworkers in Boston, reported that these girls had elevated urinary gonadotropins, thus demonstrating that their sexual infantilism was due to primary gonadal failure rather than hypo-pituitarism as had been suggested by Henry Turner in 1938. To learn more about their gonadal failure Wilkins persuaded Richard Te Linde, the chief of gynecology to explore the pelvis in five such patients.

He found that the gonads in all patients consisted only of fibrous streaks composed exclusively of ovarian stromal cells.

There were no germ cells or ovarian follicles, although there were occasional mesonephric remnants.

In his classic 1944 paper, Wilkins reported his findings and pointed out that studies of patients with streak gonads might provide powerful evidence supporting or refuting the various theories of sex differentiation. He critically evaluated each of the theories that had been advanced, including that of Weisner who believed that in the absence of fetal gonadal secretions all embryos would be feminine, although androgen could influence male differentiation.

1949 Meeting with Alfred Jost

The classic studies of Jost on the fetal castration in rabbits are very well-known now. They demonstrated that the fetal testis is necessary for differentiation as a male, but in the absence of fetal gonads both the internal and external genitalia developed as a normal female. In 1949, Jost presented his findings on sex differentiation to an International Congress of Gynecology in Mexico City. On the way home, he arranged to visit the Carnegie Institute of Embryology in Baltimore, which housed Streeter and Corner, the leading human embryologists of the day. After hearing Jost's story, the embryologists insisted that he meet Dr. Wilkins who had a healthy interest in the hormonal control of sex differentiation.

Twenty-five years later, Jost recalled the encounter:

"He was fifty-five and I was thirty-three and not even a doctor of medicine. He calmly and patiently followed my description of the rabbit experiments and asked many penetrating questions. He then showed me his portfolio of clinical cases of sexual ambiguity asking me to help him interpret the pathophysiology. The discussions went on for many hours into the late afternoon and Dr. Wilkins finally concluded, 'I am convinced that if what you say is true, half of my beautiful girls with ovarian agenesis are really boys!'"

Unfortunately there was no way to determine genetic sex at that time. Nevertheless, Wilkins felt sufficiently secure with this interpretation that he cited this hypothesis as a footnote in his 1950 textbook.

Four or five years after Lawson's encounter with Alfred Jost, when Mel Grumbach and I were fellows of Wilkins, we reported in journal club that a Canadian pathologist, named Murray Barr, had discovered a cytological marker in nuclei of female cells but not in male cells. Lawson immediately phoned Murray Barr and arranged for him to analyze skin biopsies from a group of our patients with what we then called ovarian agenesis.

In 1954, we reported that six of eight patients lacked the chromatin dot and presumably were "genetic XY males."(91) Grumbach followed up on this and became a world authority on sex differentiation.(87)

In the 1960s, Malcolm Ferguson-Smith and Barbara Migeon did the karyotypes of the patients showing that most of them had only one X-chromosome.

Wilkins later modified his nomenclature to include various forms of the syndrome under the umbrella designation, "Syndrome of Gonadal Dysgenesis." He stoutly maintained, however, that this syndrome should never have been designated "Turner Syndrome."

The Syndrome of Testicular Feminization
Androgen Insensitivity Syndrome (AIS)

In his 1950 textbook, Wilkins described another kind of sexual ambiguity. She was an attractive thirty-year-old woman who had never menstruated and who lacked sexual hair. Surgical exploration of her pelvis revealed absence of uterus, but presence of testes and rudiments of epididymis and vas deferens.

Her urinary 17 ketosteroids ranged between 15 and 20 mg/24 hr. and her androgens measured by bioassay were similarly high for a female but normal for a male.

Wilkins treated her with methyl testosterone, up to 50 mg/day with no discernable effect on seborrhea, sexual hair, or clitoral enlargement. He therefore postulated that all of her findings were due to resistance to androgen action at the peripheral level. He called these patients "hairless ladies with testes." Several other patients were followed later. Their karyotypes were shown to be 46 XY with a plasma testosterone level usually above normal male range. The locus of the gene for the androgen receptor was determined by Drs. Meyer W., Migeon B., and Migeon C. The gene itself was isolated by Drs. D.B. Lubahn, T.R. Brown, J.A. Simental, H.N. Higgs, C.J. Migeon, E.M. Wilson, and F.S. French.

The name of testicular feminization was changed to androgen insensitivity syndrome by Money J. and Migeon C.

Unfortunately, Wilkins's observation including the correct pathophysiology of the syndrome, published in 1950 in his textbook, was ignored and the disorder was called Swyer's Syndrome for a while.

Wilkins made many other seminal contributions to Pediatric Endocrinology during the short time that he was engaged in a full-time academic career. Perhaps his single contribution that brought the nascent field of Pediatric Endocrinology into prominence was his poster session at the Sixth International Congress of Pediatrics in Zurich in 1950. This extensive display provided examples of each of the now common endocrine disorders in Pediatrics along with a delineation of diagnostic criteria and pathophysiologic basis, insofar as it was then known. This display was the foundation of his text, *Disorders of Endocrine Secretions in Childhood and Adolescence.* (84) Many European pediatricians came to Baltimore to study under Wilkins and on returning home, they founded the European Society of Pediatric Endocrinology (ESPE). Although the number of American postdoctoral fellows was not large, they and their fellows have made a very large impact on the development of Pediatric Endocrinology in America. Robert Blizzard and Claude Migeon, who succeeded Wilkins as co-directors of Pediatric Endocrinology at Harriett Lane honored their former chief by establishing an annual symposium in his name, and this symposium evolved into the Lawson Wilkins Pediatric Endocrine Society (LWPES).

The legacy left by Wilkins to the discipline of Pediatric Endocrinology is indeed remarkable for an individual who remained in the private practice of Pediatrics until well after his fiftieth birthday!

I have often wondered whether Wilkins should be included in the pantheon of great scientists. The word science comes from the Greek work "scio," which means "to know." Wilkins's major tool was insatiable curiosity—he could not stand not knowing. His curiosity led to great things, and I do not hesitate to classify him among the great scientists of all time.

Fellows of the Pediatric Endocrine Clinic, 1938-1963 (Figures 31-39)

Associates and Fellows from the United States

Walter Fleischmann	1938-1946
Roger A. Lewis	1946-1950
Robert Klein	1948-1950
Eugenia Rosemberg	1948-1950
Lytt I. Gardner	1950-1952
John F. Crigler, Jr.	1950-1951
Claude J. Migeon	1950-1952
Samuel H. Silverman	1951-1952
John Money	1950-1952
Alfred M. Bongiovanni	1952-1954
Walter R. Eberlein	1952-1953
George W. Clayton	1952-1954
Melvin M. Grumbach	1953-1955
Thomas Shepard III	1954-1955
Judson J. Van Wyk	1953-1955
Robert M. Blizzard	1955-1957
H. David Mosier, Jr.	1955-1957
David W. Smith	1955-1956
Gerald H. Holman	1956-1958
Robert S. Stempfel, Jr.	1956-1958
Orville C. Green	1957-1960
Gloria Steward	1957
William W. Cleveland	1958-1960
Heskel M. Haddad	1958-1959
Malcolm M. Martin	1958
Raphael R. David	1958-1961
Thomas Aceto, Jr.	1960-1962
Alvro M. Camacho	1960-1962
Frederic M. Kenny	1960-1962

Wellington Hung	1960-1962
James Wright	1961-1964
Jordan W. Finkelstein	1961-1963
JoAnne Brasel	1962-1965
Avinoam Kowarski	1962-1965
John S. Spaulding	1962-1964

Figure 31. A few months before his death), Lawson Wilkins called a meeting of his past fellows. Front row, from left: Drs. James Wright, John Gerrard,Walter Eberlein, George Clayton, Jordan Finkelstein, Robert Klein. Second row:Drs. Robert Blizzard, Eugenia Rosemberg, Walter Fleischmann, Lawson Wilkins, JoAnne Brasel, Bernadette Loras, John Money, Barbara Migeon. Third Row: Drs. William Cleveland, Alfred Bongiovanni, John Spaulding, Raphael David, Avinoam Kowarski, Claude Migeon, Frederic Kenny, Judson Van Wyk, David Alexander,Melvin Grumbach, Malcolm Martin, John Crigler, Robert Stempfel, David Mosier. Fourth Row: Drs. Donald Delahaye, Buford Nichols Jr., Charles Snipes, Wellington Hung, Orville Green, Thomas Aceto Jr (1963).

Fellows from Abroad

Salvador de Majo	Argentina	1948-1950
Gordon Kennedy	England	1951-1952
Jose Cara	Argentina	1951-1952
Henning Andersen	Denmark	1953
Constantine Papadatos	Greece	1954
Edouard Juillard	Switzerland	1955
John Gerrard	England	1956
Donald J. Delahaye	Canada	1956-1957
Fouad Hamaoui	Lebanon	1957
David Alexander	Scotland	1958-1960
Jean Bertrand	France	1955-1956
Jean-Luc de Gennes	France	1957
Cesar Bergada	Argentina	1959-1961
John P. Eckert	Australia	1959-1961
Enrico Delanto	Mexico	1959
Raphael Rappaport	France	1960-1961
Marija Nikesic	Yugoslavia	1960
Paul Malvaux	Belgium	1961-1962
Bernadette Loras	France	1962-1964
Marco A. Rivarola	Argentina	1963-1967
Dagfinn Aarskog	Norway	1960-1962
Morato Morano	Uruguay	1961-1962

57

LEGACY OF LAWSON WILKINS: THE FELLOWS

D r. Wilkins was not only one of the major creators of the new field of Pediatric Endocrinology but he was also a major mentor of trainees of this field.

Dr. Melvin Grumbach from the University of California in San Francisco analyzed in a sensitive statement what made Dr. Wilkins a great man. He stated the following:

> Lawson was a man for all seasons, a many-sided man, clinician, scientist, mentor, educator, encyclopedist, recorder, raconteur and a pioneer who fathered and fostered the academic and clinical discipline of Pediatric Endocrinology. He cast a large shadow.
>
> Lawson had a restless, inquiring mind, and insatiable curiosity. He was a great clinician but he was also a great scientist—not a bench scientist but a clinical investigator whose laboratory was the clinic, bedside, and operating room. Soon after founding the Endocrine Clinic at Harriet Lane Home, he recruited a series of gifted laboratory directors. They were able to bring to bear the most recent advances in laboratory techniques on the research questions at hand and served as laboratory mentors for a covey of fledgling fellows. Lawson had a profound understanding of the scientific method and the rules of evidence. A keen observer, with an extraordinary ordered mind, meticulous data collector and recorder, he instilled in all of us the importance of attention to detail whether in clinical observations or laboratory work.

Lawson was a hypothesis tester and a critical one. To convince him of the validity of a clinical or laboratory findings or the evidence in favor of particular speculation, one had to do more than one's homework. A born doubter, his acceptance did not come easily. Parenthetically, he gave little credence to idle speculation or ideas, hypotheses or notions that were not susceptible to testing.

Once Lawson developed an interest in a clinical problem, he explored it with great determination, commitment, and thought. He had a contagious enthusiasm and the ability to interest others skilled in the laboratory to address clinical problems. He read widely, and freely discussed the clinical issues that interested him with a wide and diverse group of scientists and clinical investigators. He was eminently approachable.

A compassionate man with a lust for life, he was intensely loyal to his fellows, "The Boys," and took great pride in their achievements. Lawson was an indefatigable worker, but he also loved a good time. Conviviality, get-togethers usually marked by song, and weekends on the Chesapeake were an important part of his and Lu's life. He was a wonderful informal host. Lawson hated to be alone and thrived on gregariousness.

Who can forget the twinkle in his eyes, the gentle smile, and the glowing cigarette held between nicotine-stained fingers, the stentorian resonant voice, his warmth and vigor and the affection, which he generated in his fellows?

Dr. Robert Blizzard, another fellow, wrote a profile of Lawson Wilkins in the *Journal of Pediatrics*. He had a section on Wilkins as a teacher. He wrote the following:

Wilkins's accomplishments as a teacher reached their pinnacle after he joined the faculty at Hopkins in 1946. He taught orally at the bedside, in the clinic and in the classroom and through the written word in his manuscripts. He documented, through photography and charts, the longitudinal manifestations of endocrine, metabolic, and dysmorphologic diseases; this led to "poster teaching sessions" at the American Academy of Pediatrics annual meetings in the late 1940s and early 1950s. Because of the favorable reception, he published this material in the first edition (1950) of his textbook entitled, *The Diagnosis and Treatment of Endocrine Disorders in Childhood and Adolescence.* His book excelled as a model teaching text because of the clarity of the writing and the case histories, which were frequently longitudinal.

The memorable Saturday endocrinology clinics were held in the Harriet Lane Home outpatient department from 9:00 a.m. to 1:00 p.m. and were attended by many residents, faculty members, fellows and students. After the patients were all seen by a fellow or resident, the presentations and discussions began. As Wilkins paced back and forth across the floor in his white coat, with hands behind his back, he discussed what was known about each patient, what was known about the patient's condition, and what was not known. As should be true of all great teachers, he welcomed thoughts, questions and comments.

The following listing of the many fellows of Lawson Wilkins and specific comments about these fellows was written in collaboration by William Cleveland and Claude Migeon. Efforts were made to be accurate but we apologize for any error or omission.

<u>Walter Fleischmann, PhD</u> (1938-1946) was born and educated in Vienna. His father, Carl, was an obstetrician, a friend of Sigmund Freud, and he delivered Anne Freud. Walter was a PhD involved in research. In 1938, he was at a conference in Chicago at the time of the Munich Agreement. He was advised to stay in the United States and Lawson Wilkins gave him a job at Johns Hopkins University.

Walter was able to bring his wife and daughter, Ruth, to the US after going to Antwerp. His parents and siblings went to England when they settled. Ruth Fleischmann Weiner wrote, "In effect, Lawson Wilkins saved the lives of the Fleischmann family."

Walter worked on the effects of various androgenic steroids on creatine metabolism in humans.(23) He was also involved in the attempt to suppress adrenal hypersecretion by various synthetic steroids, unfortunately with effect until cortisone was used. He joined the Veteran Administration Hospital of Baltimore and, later worked in Tennessee.

Roger Lewis, MD (1946-1950) was involved with the clinic collaborating with colleagues who carried out several studies of thyroid function and started the treatment of children with congenital adrenal hyperplasia. (35)

Eugenia Rosemberg, MD (1948-1950) came from Argentina and worked with Roger Lewis and Robert Klein, helping the investigation of the patients with congenital adrenal hyperplasia. (52) When she left, she went to the NIH and later joined the steroid group in Shrewsbury, Massachusetts, with Dr. Gregory Pincus. Dr. Gregory Pincus and Dr. M.C. Chang were the first to synthesize the combined oral contraceptive pill. Later, Eugenia established her Pediatric Endocrine Clinic at the Worchester Hospital.

Salvatore de Majo, MD (1948-1950) graduated from medical school in Buenos Aires. He came to learn at the clinic and the treatment of its patients. In addition, he worked with Dr. Lewis on the effects of ovariectomy on albino rats, as well as on the effects of various synthetic steroids on the rat adrenals. When he returned home, he became the director of the Pediatric Endocrine Clinic at the Hospital de Niños in Buenos Aires.

Robert Z. Klein, MD (1948-1950) graduated from the Harvard Medical School and had training in pediatrics at the Boston Children's Hospital. He was an instructor at Johns Hopkins working in Endocrinology with Wilkins and was co-author of some of the pioneering publications about adrenal hyperplasia. (54-55) He left Hopkins for the University of Pittsburgh where he established a highly regarded program in Endocrinology, continuing research and training fellows. He subsequently held professorships at Boston University and Dartmouth. He continued to make valuable contributions particularly in the area of measuring outcome in congenital hypothyroidism and its relationship to treatment. In this work, he directed the New England Congenital Hypothyroidism Collective.

Figure 32. Lawson Wilkins and the fellows. From left: Jose Cara, Claude Migeon, Lawson Wilkins, Gordon Kennedy and George Clayton. (1951-1952)

Lytt Gardner, MD (1950-1952) was originally from North Carolina and could make the best julep in the world. He directed the laboratories at Hopkins and contributed to the work on congenital adrenal hyperplasia. (66) He established a pediatric endocrine program at the new State University of New York Upstate Medical Center in Syracuse where he remained until his death in 1986. He was succeeded by Dr. Robert A. Richman. Dr. Gardner's life, professional career and many valuable contributions have been described by Dr. Mary L. Voorhees (former fellow), and includes a notable list of pediatric endocrinologists trained by Gardner. His work resulted in a highly respected textbook, Endocrine and Genetic Diseases of Childhood and Adolescence.

John F. Crigler, Jr., MD (1950-1951) was a member of the house staff at Johns Hopkins. Prior to joining the Wilkins group, he was co-author of many of the early papers on treatment of adrenal hyperplasia with cortisone. (63) He then went to Boston Children's Hospital as a member of the faculty of the Harvard Medical School. He established a very productive endocrinology division. His training program included seventy fellows from all over the world. John remained in this position until his retirement.

Claude J. Migeon, MD (1950-1952) completed his medical education and pediatric residency in Paris, France. A Fulbright Fellowship brought him to Lawson Wilkins for two years. (60, 62) After three very productive years with Leo T. Samuels in Salt Lake City studying cortisol secretion and metabolism in humans, he returned to Johns Hopkins, and stayed there for the rest of his long career. In 1960, he was named the Co-Director of the Pediatric Endocrine Clinic with Robert Blizzard and was named Director in 1974 until 1994. During these 30 years, he had many fellows from the US and abroad.

John Money, Ph.D. (1951) led a group studying the psychologic factors involved in pediatric endocrine disorders. Other valuable contributions to this group came from the John and Joan Hampson.(99, 110) When John Money was asked how he came to Johns Hopkins, he responded as follows:

> In 1949-1950, as a graduate student at Harvard, I had a student appointment at Massachusetts General Hospital, writing a dissertation on the psychosexuality of hermaphroditism. Fuller Albright and Fred Bartter arranged for me to meet Lawson Wilkins when he attended the American Academy of Pediatrics annual meeting in Boston and gave his popular workshop on the adrenogenital syndrome of female pseudohermaphroditism. The efficacy of cortisone, newly synthesized for the treatment of the syndrome was simultaneously confirmed at MGH and Johns Hopkins in the first week of 1950.

Lawson and I got along well professionally, perhaps because I had already resolved to use pediatric not psychoanalytic English. He approved my request to visit Hopkins to abstract psychological information from the files of patients whose cases had been published by hospital number, and to interview maybe one or two of them for my dissertation. When the written letter of invitation arrived however, it was to invite me to work in the pediatric endocrine clinic full time. I began in July 1951.

It has always seemed remarkable to me that this very pragmatic, chart-making man, not much given to psychologizing, should have had the prescience to recognize that he was on to something basically very important psychologically in treating people with hormones.

Although I was not a postdoctoral fellow in pediatric endocrinology, Lawson Wilkins provided me, especially at the famed Saturday clinic, with as much pediatric endocrinology as I needed to become the first pediatric psychoendocrinologist. Here resides the outstanding feature of his intellectual and academic grandeur as it most personally affected me.

I think that Lawson Wilkins metaphorically adopted all of his trainees, his "boys" (this was not the age of equal opportunity), as substitutes for his only son whom he lost at age sixteen in a postal truck auto accident. Double-twisting the helix, he had also himself become a stand in for his son, starting a new career as if on his son's behalf. Confronting his loss, he gave up general pediatrics and became a full-time pediatric endocrinologist. In a sense, he was on an equal footing with his fellows as one of us, not an overbearing father, but a Socratic teacher.

Sam Silverman, MD (1951-1952) was interested only in clinical studies. He got involved with the special form of congenital adrenal hyperplasia, the hypertensive form and the salt-losing form. He also studied "Precocious Adrenarche."(65) He left Baltimore to go into practice at Pediatric Endocrinology in New Jersey.

Alfred M. Bongiovanni, MD (1952-1955) and Walter Eberlein, MD (1952-1953) became well known for their contributions to the study of abnormal secretion of adrenal steroids in the various forms of congenital adrenal hyperplasia.(75,82) They returned to Philadelphia to establish a Division of Pediatric Endocrinology. Eventually, Dr. Bongiovanni became Professor and Chairman at the Department of Pediatrics at the University of Pennsylvania from 1963 to 1972. Following this, he became an itinerant professor holding posts at the University of Ife, Nigeria, Cairo and the Catholic University of Ponce-de-Leon in Puerto Rico. He later became Dean of this school. He then returned to the faculty of the University of Pennsylvania in 1980 where he remained until his death in 1984.

George W. Clayton, MD (1952-1954) helped Dr. Bongiovanni as shown by a series of publications.(81,83) Clayton returned to his beloved Texas where he established a program at Baylor College of Medicine in Houston. He was Professor of Pediatrics and director of the Endocrine Division until his retirement. He moved to Galveston and his principal activities relate to fishing, traveling and his ongoing interest in the history of the Civil War.

Figure 33. The entrance of the Harriet Lane Home. Front, from left: Judson Van Wyk, Lawson Wilkins and Melvin Grumbach. Back: Thomas Shepard and Claude Migeon (1955-1956)

<u>Melvin M. Grumbach, MD</u> (1953-1955) was busy and very productive. He made a team with Dr. Judson Van Wyk, so their publications were conjoint. (90,92,101) The main contributions were related to the study of sex chromosomes in ovarian agenesis and a genetic study of congenital adrenal hyperplasia with Dr. Barton Childs.

He left Baltimore to head a division of Pediatric Endocrinology at Babies Hospital in New York. Among the many fellows he trained, one of the most outstanding was Selna Kaplan. When Dr. Grumbach moved to a position at the University of California at San Francisco, Selna went with him. An outstanding division has flourished as a result of their efforts. Many leading endocrinologists have been trained in their program.

Mel became chairman of the Department of Pediatrics at UCSF until his retirement. Distinguished colleagues have included Selna, Felix Conte and Walter L. Miller.

<u>Judson J. Van Wyk, MD</u> (1953-1955) was one of Wilkins's most devoted disciples. Jud was involved with Grumbach and Bongiovanni in lab work during his fellowship.(80a,81,91) He left for the University of North Carolina, where he started a vigorous Clinic of Pediatric Endocrinology. His colleagues at UNC included Frank French, Joseph D'Ercole and more recently Louis Underwood who assumed direction of the Division. Dr. Van Wyk trained many fellows including Dr. Stockholm. He made many important contributions, particularly in his work relating to somatomedin (IGF-I) as a growth factor.

Figure 34. A dinner at Old Point Comfort organized by the fellows in honor of the Wilkins family. Front, from left: Lytt Gardner, Mrs. Crigler, Lawson Wilkins, Mrs. Wilkins, Mrs. Klein and Robert Klein. Back: Walter Eberlein, John Crigler, Claude Migeon, Judson Van Wyk, Alfred Bongiovanni, Melvin Grumbach and Thomas Shepard. (1956)

<u>Thomas H. Shepard, MD</u> (1954-1955) moved to Seattle after completion of a year with Wilkins where he was appointed to the faculty at the University of Washington. He directed a division of Pediatric Endocrinology at the Children's Orthopedic Hospital from 1956-1961. He developed an interest in embryology and teratology; studies in this area became the main focus of his career. After a year as a research associate in embryology in the Department of Anatomy, University of Florida College of Medicine, he spent another six months in the Fetal Laboratory, University of Copenhagen with Dr. Henning Anderson.

Upon his return to Seattle, he continued his academic career and headed a birth defects research laboratory for thirty years. He became emeritus professor in 1993. He published extensively—some reports involving Endocrinology but most related to embryology and teratology.

Robert M. Blizzard, MD (1955-1957) was destined to play a major role in the Harriet Lane program and in Pediatric Endocrinology.(123,138,159,180) After his training, he left Hopkins to direct a division at Ohio State in Columbus. Upon Wilkins's retirement in 1960, Bob was chosen to succeed him as Clinical Director of the Harriet Lane Program with Claude Migeon as Laboratory Director. He was asked to serve as acting Chairman of the Department of Pediatrics at Hopkins following the departure of Dr. Robert Cooke. He did this for fifteen months until the position was taken over by Dr. Littlefield.

Later, Bob was recruited to the Chairmanship of the Department of Pediatrics at the University of Virginia in Charlottesville, a position which he held until his retirement. During his tenure as chairman, he maintained a productive career in Endocrinology, working with outstanding colleagues including Alan Rogol and Anne Johanson. In his "retirement," he remains very productive with many roles including chairmanship of the Board of the Genentech Foundation.

Figure 35. Lawson Wilkins among his fellows, wearing white. From left: Robert Stempfel, Gloria Steward, Claude Migeon and Gerald Holman, with John Money,far right, and his fellow, far left. (1957-1958)

Gerald H. Holman, MD (1956-1958) became a peripatetic professor after completing his residency and fellowship at Hopkins.(132) He spent 1958-1961 in Saskatoon and 1961-1964 in Kansas City. From 1964-1969, he was Professor and Chairman at the Medical College of Georgia. From 1969-1974, he was Professor and Head of Pediatrics at the University of Calgary. From 1974-1975, he was Professor and Chairman at Eastern Virginia School of Medicine. From 1975-1979, he was Dean at Norfolk. He then went to Amarillo, Texas, and held various administrative and faculty positions there, including directing a division of Pediatric Endocrinology. In these various situations, he participated in a prestigious number of programs and committees. His publications are expectedly wide ranging including Endocrinology, nutrition, ethics and the social aspects of medical care.

Robert Stempfel, MD (1956-1958) went from the training program(117,124) to appointment in the Department of Pediatrics, Duke University, School of Medicine as director of Pediatric Endocrinology. He maintained a clinical and laboratory program until his recruitment to the Chairmanship of Pediatrics at the newly established University of California School of Medicine at Davis. His involvement in Endocrinology there was somewhat peripheral. He recruited Dr. Bagher Sheikholislam to his faculty; Bagher continues in the program there. In 1971, Stempfel was enticed to come to Miami as Director of the Mailman Center for Child Development, Professor of Pediatrics and Associate Chairman. He maintained this position until 1995. During his tenure he became heavily involved in the political aspects of childcare in the State of Florida and represented the School of Medicine, University of Miami, in Tallahassee in legislative matters. After giving up directorship of the Center he moved from Miami to Key Largo and maintained his political representation until 1995 when he retired completely. He was able to devote his full attention to his abiding interest in fishing in the Keys and the Bahamas.

Orville C. Green, MD (1957-1960) left Baltimore(151,160,187) to establish a program at the Children's Memorial Hospital in the Department of Pediatrics, School of Medicine, Northwestern University. He maintained a flourishing division, productive both in research and training until his retirement. He currently spends winters in Sarasota and summers in Wilmette and Nantucket. Among his trainees was Dr. Robert Winters who has succeeded Orville in the direction of the division. When asked about Lawson Wilkins, Orville recalled two statements made by Wilkins:

1. Never take money from a drug company—take their products for experimentation if they seem worthwhile but never take money—they will never get off your back.
2. The clinical use of the science of endocrinology is to diagnose and treat conditions of excess and deficiency.
    Orville adds, "I think this basic principle should be reaffirmed."

Gloria Steward, MD (1957) left the program after six months.

David H. Mosier, Jr., MD (1955-1957) was from Kansas. He went to the University of Notre Dame and Johns Hopkins Medical School. After a Pediatric Residency at the University of Southern California, he came back to Hopkins as a fellow in Pediatric Endocrinology with Wilkins.(122,123) Afterwards, he returned to California, where he was named Professor of Pediatrics at the University of California, Irvine. As head of the Division of Endocrinology, he has been active in experimental and clinical research of the various problems influencing growth.

David W. Smith, MD (1955-1956) spent two years in the United States Army after completing his residency in Pediatrics. He returned after two years to complete one year of fellowship with Wilkins in Endocrinology. (114) He then spent a year in practice in Los Gatos, California, before accepting a faculty appointment at the University of Wisconsin. He established an Endocrinology training program producing third-generation fellows including Dr. Arlan Rosenbloom. He then took a sabbatical in Zurich and became interested in genetics. Like his mentor, he then proceeded to pioneer a new field, dysmorphology, and published the definitive text on the subject: "Recognizable Patterns of Human Malformation," which has continued as the authoritative compendium of dysmorphic syndromes. In 1966, he moved to the University of Washington where he remained as Professor of Pediatrics until his untimely death at the age of fifty-five years. His character and contributions are described in an introduction to a Festschrift issue of the *Journal of Pediatrics* in 1982.

William W. Cleveland, MD (1958-1961) left the position of Assistant Professor at the University of Miami to come to Johns Hopkins as fellow with Lawson Wilkins. He worked diligently with patients and wrote several papers. (156,178) William was also a close friend; he and his wife were our witnesses at my marriage to Barbara in 1960.

Cleveland returned to his faculty position at the fledgling School of Medicine, University of Miami. He continued to direct a Division of Endocrinology for the ensuing thirty-six years. During twenty of those years (1969-1989), he was also Chairman of the rapidly expanding Department of Pediatrics.

Malcolm M. Martin, MD (1958-1959) was originally from England. He helped review the question of pituitary dwarfism. He then went to Georgetown University in Washington, DC, where he directed the endocrine clinic.

Figure 36. The Pediatric Endocrine Clinic. Front, from left: William Cleveland, Lawson Wilkins, Orville Green, John Money. Back: Claude Migeon, Raphael David, John Eckert, David Alexander, Cesar Bergada. (1959)

Raphael David, MD (1958-1962) was educated in the French system of Cairo. He migrated to the United States and was a Hopkins pediatric resident before joining the clinic of Lawson Wilkins.(132,165,197) At the time of Wilkins's first heart attack, Ralph was his constant companion in the Marburg Building. With time, they grew very friendly.

Ralph has devoted his career to an excellent Division of Endocrinology in the Department of Pediatrics at the School of Medicine at New York University. His program has been highly productive in training and research. As might be expected from his urbane nature, he is a confirmed and enthusiastic New Yorker.

David Alexander, MD (1958-1960) was originally from Scotland. He did his pediatric residency at Johns Hopkins. After residency, he joined the Pediatric Endocrine Clinic. Following one year of clinical work, he went with his

Scottish countryman, Dr. Malcolm Ferguson-Smith, in cytogenetics. Malcolm was an expert in the investigation of karyotypes in patients. Another notable accomplishment during training of David was to marry Jean, another Hopkins pediatric resident. They moved to Kingston, Ontario, from Baltimore where they have maintained practices, David in Endocrinology and Jean in child development.

Cesar Bergada, MD (1959-1961) and his wife Estela came from prominent families in Buenos Aires. Cesar worked with Dr. Salvador de Majo and Dr. Martin Cullen. Cesar and Estela met Lawson when Lawson and his family visited South America in 1957. As a fellow, Cesar was involved in the study of DSD (intersex) patients in collaboration with Dr. Howard Jones in Gynecology. (178,179)

Upon completion of his training in Baltimore, Cesar returned to Buenos Aires to establish an endocrine division at the Hospital de Niños R. Gutierrez, which he directed for more than three decades. Cesar was recognized as one of the outstanding pediatric endocrinologists in South America. He has trained many endocrinologists, including his own son and Marco Rivarola.

Thomas Aceto, Jr., MD (1960-1962) left the army in 1960 to join the training program at Hopkins, along with Alvro Camacho and Fritz Kenny.(173) After that, he went to the Children's Hospital of University of Buffalo. Then he became the Chairman of Pediatrics at the University of South Dakota at Sioux Falls. His next promotion was as Medical Director of the Cardinal Glennon Memorial Hospital at St. Louis University. Unfortunately, Thomas developed Alzheimer's disease and died in 2009.

Figure 37. The fellows at work. Top left: Paul Malvaux using paper chromatography. Top right: Alvro Camacho checking the fraction collector. Bottom left: James Wright preparing solutions for column chromatography. Bottom right: Fritz Kenny and the spectrophotometer. (1961-1962)

Frederic M. Kenny, MD (1960-1962) graduated from Princeton. He attended Hopkins for medical school and pediatric resident training. He married Jean, a colleague in resident training. For two years (1958-1960) he was Pediatrician in Chief at the US Naval Hospital in Annapolis.

In 1960, he returned to Hopkins for two very busy years in Pediatric Endocrinology.(186,200,204) Next, he moved to the Children's Hospital at the University of Pittsburgh. There, he took the place of Dr. Robert Klein and worked at a very large diabetes clinic, which attracted other Hopkins fellows, Dr. Alan Drash and Dr. Dorothy Becker. Unfortunately, Fritz battled with depression and ended his own life in 1978.

Wellington Hung, MD (1960-1962) did most of his training and spent most of his life in Washington, DC, at American University, the Medical School of George Washington University and the Children's Hospital of DC.

After two years at Hopkins doing clinical research, he returned to Children's Hospital, National Medical Center, Washington, DC.

During his stay at Hopkins, he had learned about thyroidology from Dr. Robert Blizzard, and he became an expert in this field.(180,181,189)

Along with colleagues Dr. August and Dr. Glasgow, he wrote a succinct book of Pediatric Endocrinology.

Dagfinn Aarskog, MD (1962-1963) did his undergraduate and medical school studies in Norway at the University of Oslo and Bergen, respectively. He did his pediatric training at the University of Bergen prior to coming to Baltimore. (196) Upon his return to Norway, he became Professor and Chairman of the University of Bergen in 1971. In 1984, he was Dean of the Faculty of Medicine. Dagfinn contributed greatly to the field of Pediatric Endocrinology, including describing the Aarskog Syndrome.

John Spaulding, MD (1962-1963) was a fellow for only one year during which he contributed to the study of patients with the rare problem of unresponsiveness of the adrenals to ACTH. After his fellowship, he rejoined the University of Kansas Medical Center where he directed the clinic of Pediatric Endocrinology.

JoAnne Brasel, MD (1962-1965) was a lovely lady who lived her life fighting a slow progressive, disabling neurological problem. She went to medical school at the University of Colorado and did her residency at Cornell University.

From 1962 to 1965, she joined the Hopkins Pediatric Endocrinology program and joined the staff in 1968. She became interested in growth and development research, working successively at Cornell, Columbia and Harbor-UCLA Medical Center. She was in charge of the training program at Harbor-UCLA. When she died in 2007, we lost a great scientist and a wonderful friend.

Jordan Finkelstein, MD (1961-1963) spent two years at Hopkins.(200) He worked with Dr. Kowarski on the determination of aldosterone secretion in rats in various conditions. Particularly, the study of patients with congenital adrenal hyperplasia showed that all of them have a salt-losing tendency, but those who had a milder mutation of their 21-hydroxylase gene could compensate with increased aldosterone secretion, therefore avoiding salt-loss. In contrast, the patients with severe mutations could not compensate and were salt-losers. Jordan returned to Montefiore Hospital in the Bronx.

A. Avinoam Kowarski, MD (1962-1965) was born in Tel Aviv, Israel. He started medical school in Lausanne, Switzerland, and finished at the Hebrew University of Jerusalem. After three years as fellow at Hopkins(198,200) and two years at Hadassah University Hospital, he returned to the pediatric endocrine clinic, where he was involved with laboratory research. In 1981, he opened the Pediatric Endocrine Clinic at the University of Maryland.

Gordon Kennedy, MD (1951-1952) came from Cambridge, England, with the purpose to see the function of the Pediatric Endocrine Clinic. He was an expert on experimental brain lesions to rats, which resulted in increased appetite and gross obesity.

José Cara, MD (1951-1952) came from Argentina. He was interested in clinical work and eventually joined Lytt Gardner at Syracuse. José's son was also an endocrinologist.

Other doctors from abroad were truly involved in all the activities of the Clinic. The first was Dr. Jean Bertrand (1955-1956) from Lyon, France. We became close friends and after his return home, he went to join me in Stockholm to help me at the Karolinska Hospital where we worked with Dr. Carl Gemzell on the transplacental passage of steroids.(171) Bernadette Loras, MD (1962-1964), Maguelone Forest, MD and José Saez, MD were three pupils of Jean Bertrand who worked in his laboratories.

Raphael Rappaport, MD (1960-1961) came from the Hopital de Enfants Malades and then returned home to create an important clinic.(183) Paul Malvaux, MD (1961-1962) came from Louvain and similarly returned to his institution to be the Director of Pediatric Endocrinology. Both of them returned to Johns Hopkins to help with the clinical load when Dr. Blizzard was temporary Chief of Pediatrics.

Some doctors who had not been fellows felt that Wilkins was their mentor. For example, Andrea Prader of Zurich, Switzerland, the founder of the European Society of Pediatric Endocrinology, wrote the following:

> Because Lawson had the greatest impact on my training as a clinician and clinical investigator, I add a personal note regarding Lawson. He, along with Guido Fanconi, stimulated my interests in endocrinology, metabolism, genetics, and growth. Both were superb clinicians and forceful and enthusiastic teachers.
>
> Their scientific contributions were not the results of systematic laboratory research in the framework of a sophisticated research program, but the offshoots of very careful clinical observations combined with a deep interest in the patient and his problems. They used charts to follow the courses of diseases and the growth of patients. They recognized important disease aspects not noted by others, were able to add new insights into many diseases and offered challenging new speculations.

Figure 38 The staff of the Pediatric Endocrine Clinic on the steps of the Harriet Lane Home. Front, from left: Bernadette Loras, Claude Migeon, Lawson Wilkins, JoAnne Brasel, Robert Blizzard, John Money, Avinoam Kowarski and Viola Lewis. Back: John Spaulding, Charles Snipes, Robert Chandler, James Wright, Jordan Finkelstein. (1962-1963)

This was the same for Henning Anderson of Denmark. Henning had a special relationship with Lawson. When they were together, Lawson and Henning considered themselves as Vikings and Harold the Blue Tooth was one of their ancestors.

Another important admirer of Lawson Wilkins was Professor Alfred Jost, head of the Laboratory of Comparative Physiology, Faculty of Sciences at the University of Paris. After Wilkins's death in 1963, Dr. Jost gave the fourth Lawson Wilkins Memorial Lecture on April 26, 1971. On that occasion, he wrote about meeting Lawson Wilkins:

> On my return from Mexico, I visited several eminent American experts in the field on sex differentiation in animals. The first stop was in Baltimore, where I was to meet world-famous scientists at the Department of Biology of The Johns Hopkins University and at the Department of Embryology of the Carnegie Institution of Washington. Dr. Robert K. Burns an Associate in Embryology was very friendly to me during this visit, and he suggested that I should meet at The Johns Hopkins Hospital a clinician by the name of Dr. Lawson Wilkins, who was interested in problems of human genital anomalies. Dr. Burns made the appointment for the early afternoon, and thus I was introduced to Lawson Wilkins. He was 55, I was 33; he was a well-known clinician, I was not even a doctor of medicine. He calmly and patiently followed my description of the rabbit experiments, looking at the rabbit pictures, asked many pertinent questions, and listened to the interpretations proposed for human anomalies. Then he submitted me to a keen clinical examination. I had to comment on the illustrations and reports concerning clinical cases. I thus had the privilege of being among the very first ones who saw the cases later to appear in the first edition of "The Diagnosis and Treatment of Endocrine Disorders in Childhood and Adolescence." But not only did I have to look at pictures, I was asked for interpretations which were coldly evaluated and screened. Also, I was introduced to extremely

important clinical experiments, for instance, those concerning the absence of sensitivity to androgens of "hairless women with testes.

Several of the fellows from abroad attended the daily clinics of Lawson Wilkins, including <u>Constantine Papadatos, MD</u> (1955) from Athens, Greece, <u>Edouard Juillard, MD</u> (1955) from Lausanne, Switzerland, <u>John Gerrard, MD</u> (1956) and <u>Donald Delahaye, MD</u> (1956) from Canada, <u>Fouad Hamaoui, MD</u> (1956) from Beirut, Lebanon, <u>Jean-Luc de Gennes, MD</u> (1957) from Paris, France, <u>Enrico Delanto, MD</u> (1959) from Mexico, <u>Marija Nikesic, MD</u> (1960) from Belgrade, Yugoslavia, <u>John Eckert, MD</u> (1961) from Australia and <u>Morato Marano, MD</u> (1962) from Montevideo, Uruguay.

Figure 39. Two great friends: Lawson Wilkins with his eternal cigarette and Henning Anderson with his pipe. (1960)

59

CONCLUSION

In 2003, on December 22, I discovered that I was eighty years old. I was amazed and a little afraid. It had been forty years since Dr. Wilkins died. I wrote a little note; a copy of which follows:

> How is it possible?
> Already eighty?
> Pas
> Possible! So many
> Years.
> But what can I do
> If it is true?
> Resign myself
> To it
> Hope for another
> Day
> And be thankful for
> My past youth

Figure 40. Claude Migeon with the portrait of Lawson Wilkins, (November 2011)

Now in 2013, we are ten years later and I am ninety years old. (Figure 40) What happened during that extra time? Well, I plan to answer that. Betsy McMaster and I have finished our memoir of Lawson Wilkins.

It is of interest to consider what role "chance" plays for better or worse in life.

In 1950, in Paris when I got my MD degree, I was not ready for settling down: get married, open an office of Pediatrics, probably in Reims and be a respectful citizen.

Chance permitted me to apply for a Fulbright Fellowship to go to a hospital in Chicago and see my good friends, Bill and Stella Nanos. Instead, chance had it that Dr. Wilkins asked for me at Hopkins. At the end of the two-year fellowship, Dr. Wilkins made it possible for me to continue working in Salt Lake City. And after three years in Utah, he brought me back to Baltimore for the rest of my life.

I want to conclude this memoir in thanking with all of my heart, Dr. Wilkins, for permitting me to have a wonderful life, with my wife Barbara, my children Jacques, Jean-Paul and Nicole; my many fellows who were like children; my kind colleagues, and all of my good friends.

58

BIBLIOGRAPHY OF THE PEDIATRIC
ENDOCRINE CLINIC
(1938-1966)

1938

1. **Wilkins, L.** The rates of growth, osseous development, and mental development in cretine as a guide to thyroid treatment. J. Pediat. 12: 429, 1938.

1939

2. **Wilkins, L.** Some problems and methods of diagnosis of cretinism and juvenile hypothyroidism. Delaware State Medical Journal, June, 1939.

1940

3. **Wilkins, L., Fleischmann, W. and Howard, J. E.** Macrogenitosomia precox associated with hyperplasia of the endrogenic tissue of the adrenal and death from the corticoadrenal insufficiency. Endocrinology 26: 385, 1940.

4. **Wilkins, L., Richter, C. P.** A great craving for salt by a child with corticoadrenal insufficiency. J.A.M.A. 114: 866, 1940.

5. **Wilkins, L.** Thyroid medication during childhood. J.A.M.A. 114: 2382, 1940.

6. Fleischmann, W., Shumacher, H. B., Jr. and Wilkins, L. The effect of thyroidectomy on serum cholesterol and basal metabolic rate in the rabbit. Am. J. Physiol. 131: 317, 1940.

1941

7. Wilkins, L. Epiphysial dysgenesis associated with hypothyroidism. Am. J. Dis. Child. 61: 13, 1941.

8. Wilkins, L., Fleischmann, W. and Block, W. Studies on hypothyroidism in childhood: (1) The basal metabolic rate, serum cholesterol and urinary creatine before treatment. J. Clin. Endocrinol. 1: 3, 1941.

9. Wilkins, L., Fleischmann, W. and Block, W. Studies on hypothyroidism in childhood: (2) Sensitivity to thyroid medication as measured by the serum cholesterol and the creatine excretion. J. Clin. Endocrinol. 1: 14, 1941.

10. Wilkins, L. and Fleischmann, W. Studies on hypothyroidism in childhood: (3) The effect of withdrawal of thyroid therapy upon the serum cholesterol. Relationship of cholesterol, basal metabolic rate, weight and clinical symptoms. J. Clin. Endocrinol. 1: 91, 1941.

11. Wilkins, L. and Fleischmann, W. Studies on hypothyroidism in childhood: (4) The creatine and cholesterol response to thyrotropic hormone. J. Clin. Endocrinol. 1: 98, 1941.

12. Hartman, Carl G. and Fleischmann, W. Serum cholesterol in the rhesus monkey. Endocrinology 29: 793, 1941.

13. Wilkins, L. Recent studies on the diagnosis of hypothyroidism in children. The Pennsylvania Medical Journal 44: 429, 1941.

14. Wilkins, L. and Fleischmann, W. The diagnosis of hypothyroidism in childhood. J.A.M.A. 116: 2459, 1941.

15. Fleischmann, W. and Wilkins, L. Sterol balance in hypothyroidism. J. Clin. Endocrinol. 1: 799, 1941.

16. **Wilkins, L., Fleischmann, W. and Howard, J. E.** Crestinuris induced by methyltestosterone in the treatment of dwarfed boys and girls. Bull. Johns Hopkins Hosp. 69: 493, 1941.

1942

17. **Fleischmann, W. and Shumacher, H. B., Jr.** The relationship between serum cholesterol and total body cholesterol in experimental hyper-and hypothyroidism. Bull. Johns Hopkins Hosp. 71: 175, 1942.
18. **Howard, J.E., Wilkins, L. and Fleischmann, W.** The metabolic and growth effects of various androgens in sexually immature dwarfs. Trans. Assn. Am. Physicians. 57: 212, 1942.

1943

19. **Fleischmann, W., Shumacher, H. B., Jr. and Straus, W. L., Jr.** Influence of age on the effect of thyroidectomy in the rhesus monkey. Endocrinology 32: 238, 1943.

1944

20. **Wilkins, L. and Fleischmann, W.** Sexual infantilism in the female: causes, diagnosis and treatment. J. Clin. Endocrinol. 4: 306, 1944.
21. **Wilkins, L. and Fleischmann, W.** Ovarian agenesis, pathology, associated clinical symptoms and the bearing on the theories of sex differentiation. J. Clin. Endocrinol. 4: 357, 1944.
22. **Frame, E. G., Fleischmann, W. and Wilkins, L.** The influence of a number of endrogenic steroids on the urinary excretion of neutral 17-ketosteroids. Bull. Johns Hopkins Hosp. 75: 95, 1944.

22a. **Fleischman, W. and Fried, Ilse E.** Studies on the hypercholesterolemia of immature fowl induced by estrogen. Fed. Proc., Vol. 3. No. I, March, 1944.

1945

23. **Wilkins, L. and Fleischmann, W.** Studies on the creatinuris due to methylated steroids. J. Clin. Invest. <u>24</u>: 21, 1945.
24. **Fleischmann, W. and Fried, I. E.** Studies on the mechanism of the hypercholesterolemis and hypercalcemia induced by estrogen in immature chicks. Endocrinology <u>36</u>: 406, 1945.

1946

24a. **Fleischmann, W.** Effect of thyroxin on estrogen-induced changes in fowl. Fed. Proc., Vol. 5, No. I, March, 1946.
25. **Wilkins, L. and Fleischmann, W.** Effects of thyroid on creatine metabolism with a discussion of the mechanism of storage and excretion of creatine bodies. J. Clin. Investigation <u>25</u>: 360, 1946.
26. **Wilkins, L.** The influence of various androgenic steroids on nitrogen balance and growth. J. Clin. Endocrinol. <u>6</u>: 383, 1946.

1947

27. **Fleischmann, W. and Breckler, I. A. With the technical assistance of Fisk, A. J.** Mitotic and wound healing activities of the corneal epithelium in thiouracel treated and thyroidectomized rats. Endocrinology <u>41</u>: 266, 1947.
27a. **Buschke, W., Friedenwald, J. S. and Fleischmann, W.** Studies on the mitotic activity of the corneal epithelium. Methods. The effects of colchicine, ether, cocaine and ephedrin. Bull. Johns Hopkins Hosp. <u>73</u>: 143, 1943.

1948

28. **Wilkins, L.** Genetic and endocrine factors in the growth and development of childhood and adolescence. Rec. Prog. Horm. Res. 2: 391, 1948.

29. **Wilkins, L.** A feminizing adrenal tumor causing gynecomastia in a boy of five years contrasted with a virilising tumor in a five year old girl. Classification of 70 cases of adrenal tumor in children according to their hormonal manifestations and a review of II cases of feminising adrenal tumor in adults. J. Clin. Endocrinol. 8: III, 1948.

30. **Wilkins, L.** Abnormalities and variations of sexual development during child hood and adolescence. Advances in Pediatrics 3: 159, 1948.

31. **Wilkins, L. and Lewis, R. A.** The renal excretion of steroid hormones in pseudohermaphroditism and male sexual precocity associated with symptoms of Addison's Disease. Trans. Conf. on Metabolic Aspects of Convalescence 17: 210, 1948.

32. **Wilkins, L. and Lewis, R. A.** The relationship of dosage and duration of treatment to adrenal atrophy caused by injection of steroid hormone. Trans. Conf. on Metabolic Aspects of Convalescence 17: 168, 1948.

33. **Gantt, W. H. and Fleischmann, W.** Effect of thyroid therapy on the conditional reflex function in hypothyroidism. Am. J. Psychiatry 104: 673, 1948.

34. **Nyda, M. J., de Majo, S. and Lewis, R. A.** The effect of ovariectomy and physiologic doses of estradiol upon body weight, linear growth and fat content of the female albine rat. Bull. Johns Hopkins Hosp. 83: 279, 1948.

1949

35. **Lewis, R. A. and Wilkins, L.** The effect of adrenocorticotropic hormone in congenital adrenal hyperplasia with virilism and in Cushing's Syndrome treated with methyltestosterone. J. Clin. Invest. 28: 394, 1949.

36. **Hardy, J. and Wilkins, L.** Methyl-testosterone in the treatment of premature infants. J. Pediat. <u>34</u>: 349, 1949.

37. **Wilkins, L.** Hyperadrenocorticism. Pediatrics <u>3</u>: 533, 1949.

38. **Lewis, R. A. and Wilkins, L.** The effects of 17-vinyl-testosterone and of other steroids upon the size and cholesterol content of the rat adrenal. Trans. Conf. on Metabolic Interrelations <u>I</u>: 159, 1949.

39. **Wilkins, L. and Lewis, R. A.** Metabolic effects of ACTH in cases of congenital adrenal hyperplasia of the adrenogenital type and in a case of Cushing's Syndrome. Trans. Conf. on Metabolic Interrelations <u>I</u>: 149, 1949.

40. **Lewis, R. A., de Majo, S. and Rosenberg, E.** The effects of 17-vinyl-testosterone upon the rat adrenal. Endocrinology <u>45</u>: 564, 1949.

<u>1950</u>

41. **Wilkins, L., Lewis, R. A. and Klein, R.** The response to ACTH in various types of adrenal hyperplasia. Trans. Armour Laboratorities Conf. on ACTH.

42. **Wilkins, L., Lewis, R. A., Klein, R. and Rosenberg, E.** Die wirkung von cortison auf die ausscheidung der 17-ketosteroids und anderer steroids bei patienten mit kongenitaler nebennierenhyperplasia. Halvetica Paediatrica Acta <u>5</u>: 418, 1950.

43. **Wilkins, L.** Nebennierenrinden-erkrankungen bein kinde. Sonderabdruck aus der Schweiserischen Medizinischen Wochenschrift. 80. Jahrgang 1950, Nr. 29, Seite 766.

44. **Wilkins, L.** Hypothyroidism in children. Prog. in Clin. Endocrinology, January, 1950.

45. **Rosenberg, E. and Lewis, R. A.** Reducation in eosinophil level of adrenalectomised mice following injection of adrenocorticotropin, 11-dehydre-17-hydroxycorticosterene and lipid extracts of human urine. J. Applied Physiology <u>3</u>: 164, 1950.

46. **Penneys, R., Thomas, C.B. and Lewis, R. A.** Reduction in the number of circulating eosinophils following induced anoxemia. Bull. Johns Hopkins Hosp. <u>86</u>: 102, 1950.

47. **Lewis, R. A., Klein, R. and Wiklins, L.** Effect of pituitary growth hormone in dwarfism with osseous retardation and hypoglycemia in a cretin treated with thyroid. J. Clin. Invest. <u>29</u>: 460, 1950.

48. **Klein, R. and Hanson, J.** Adrenocortical function in the new-born infant as measured by adrenocorticotropic hormone-eosinophil response. Pediatrics <u>6</u>: 192, 1950.

49. **Lewis, R. A., Klein, R. and Wilkins, L.** Congenital adrenal hyperplasia with pseudohermaphroditism and symptoms of Addison's disease; clinical course following bilateral total adrenalectomy with metabolic studies, pathological findings and discussion of etiology. J. Clin. Endocrinol. <u>10</u>: 703, 1950.

50. **Schoenbach, E. B., Colsky, J. and Lewis, R. A.** Steroid excretion in patients receiving anti-folic acid compounds. Cancer <u>3</u>: 844, 1950.

51. **Wilkins, L.** Round Table Discussion of Endocrine Therapy in Childhood. Pediatrics <u>6</u>: 908, 1950.

52. **Wilkins, L., Lewis, R. A., Klein, R. and Rosenberg, E.** The suppression of androgen secretion by cortisone in a case of congenital adrenal hperplasia. Bull. Johns Hopkins Hosp. <u>86</u>: 249, 1950.

53. **Lewis, R. A. and Rosenberg, E.** The effects of 17-hydroxy-11-dehydrocorticosterone upon the adrenals of normal and hypophysectomized rats maintained with adrenocorticotropin. Endocrinology <u>47</u>: 414, 1950.

54. **Klein, R. and Livingstone, S.** The effect of adrenocorticotropic hormone in epilepsy. J. Pediat. <u>37</u>: 733, 1950.

<u>1951</u>

55. **Klein, R.** Adrenocortical control of sodium and potassium excretion in the newborn. J. Clin. Invest. <u>30</u>: 318, 1951.

56. **Wilkins, Lawson and (by invitation) Gardner, Lytt I., Crigler, John F., Jr. and Migeon, Claude J.** Treatment of congenital adrenal hyperplasia with cortisone. Trans. Assn. Am. Physicians <u>64</u>: 160, 1951.

57. **Gardner, L. I., Crigler, J. F., Jr. and Migeon, C. J.** The inhibition of urinary 17-ketosteroid excretion produced by "Benemid." Proc. Soc. Ex. Biol. & Med. <u>78</u>: 460, 1951.

58. Wilkins, L., Lewis, R. A., Klein, R., Gardner, L. I., Crigler, J. F., Jr., Rosemberg, E. and Migeon, C. J. Treatment of congenital adrenal hyperplasia with cortisone. J. Clin. Endocrocrinol. 11: I, 1951.

59. Gardner, L. I. and Migeon, C. J. Le diagnostic des tumeurs virilisantes du cortex surrenalien: effet de la cortisone sur les steroides urinatres et utilisantion d'une methode colorimetrique pour le dosage de la dehydroisoandrosterone. Halvetica Paediatrica Acta 6: 465, 1951

1952

60. Wilkins, L., Gardner, L. I., Crigler, J. F., Jr., Silverman, S. H. and Migeon, C.J. Further studies on the treatment of congenital adrenal hyperplasia with cortisone. I. Comparison of oral and intramuscular administration of cortisone, with a note on the suppressive action of comounds F and B on the adrenal. J. Clin. Endocrinol. & Metab. 12: 257, 1952.

61. Ibid: II. The effects of cortisone on sexual and somatic development, with an hypothesis concerning the mechanism of feminisation. J. Clin. Endocrinol. & Metab. 12: 277, 1952.

62. Wilkins, L., Crigler, J. F., Jr., Silverman, S. H., Gardner, L. I. and Migeon, C. J. Further studies on the treatment of congenital adrenal hyperplasia with cortisone. III. The control of hypartension with cortisone, with a discussion of variations in the type of congenital adrenal hyperplasia and report of a case with probable defect of carbohydrate-regulating hormones. J. Clin. Endocrinol. & Metab. 12: 1015, 1952

63. Crigler, J.F., Jr., Silverman, S.H. and Wilkins, L. Further studies on the treatment of congenital adrenal hyperplasia with cortisone. IV. The effect of cortisone and compound B in infants with disturbed electrolyte metabolism. Pediatrics 10: 397, 1952.

64. Wilkins, L. and Ravitch, N. Adrenocortical tumor arising in liver of 3 year old boy with signs of virilism and Cushing's Syndrome. Pediatrics 9: 671, 1952.

65. **Silverman, S. H., Migeon, C. J., Rosenberg, E. and Wilkins, L.** Precocious growth of sexual hair without other secondary sexual development. "Premature Pubarche" a constitutional variation of adolescence. Pediatrics 10: 426, 1952.
66. **Gardner, L. I., Migeon, C. J., Crigler, J.F., Jr., Silverman, S. H. and Wilkins, L.** Urinary dehydroisoandrosterone in hyperadrenocorticism. J. Clin. Endocrinol. & Metab. 12: 1117, 1952.
67. **Migeon, C. J. and Gardner, L. I.** Urinary estrogens (measured fluorometrically and biologically) in hyperadrenocorticism: influence of cortisone, compound F, compound B and ACTH. J. Clin. Endocrinol. & Metab. 12: 1513, 1952.
68. **Migeon, C. J., Gardner, L. I., Crigler, J. F., Jr. and Wilkins, L.** Effect of cortisone treatment for 28 days on radio-iodine metabolism in normal rats and adrenalectomised rats maintained with desoxycorticosterone. Endocrinology 51: 117, 1952.
69. **Migeon, C. J.** Effect of cortisone on lipids of serum, liver and testes in intact and adrenalectomised rats. Proc. Soc. Exper. Biol. Med. 80: 571, 1952.
70. **Wilkins, L.** Constitutional variations of adolescent development. The Mississippi Doctor. Sept., 1952, p. 107.
71. **Wilkins, L.** The diagnosis of the adrenogenital syndrome and its treatment with cortisone. J. Pediat. 41: 860, 1952.

1953

72. **Migeon, C. J.** Fractionation by countercurrent distribution of urinary estrogens in normal individuals and in patients with hyperadrenocorticism. J. Clin. Endocrinol. & Metab. 13: 674, 1953.
73. **Wilkins, L.** Disturbance in growth. Bull. N. Y. Acad. Med. 29: 280, 1953.
73a. **Wilkins, L.** Dwarfism in Current Therapy.
73b. **Wilkins, L.** Abnormalities of sexual development in children and adolescents "Seminar" of Sharp & Dohms, Oct., 1952.

73c. **Fleischmann, W.** Zur hormonal therapie des hypophysaren infantilisms beim Weibe-Mitterlung eines durch strumn lymphomatose Komplizierten Felles. Wiener Klin. Wchschr. 35: 630, 1952.

74. **Bongiovanni, A. M.** The detection of pregnandiol and pregnantrial in the urine of patients with adrenal hyperplasia. Suppression with cortisone. Bull. Johns Hopkins Hosp. 92: 244, 1953.

1954

75. **Bongiobanni, A. M., Eberlein, W. R and Cara, Jose.** Studies on the metabolism of adrenal steroids in the adrenogenital syndrome. J. Clin. Endocrinol. & Metab. 14: 409, 1954.

76. **Eberlein, W. R.** Aminoaciduris in childhood: cystinuria and cystinosis. Am. J. Med. Sciences 225: 677, 1953.

77. **Silverman, S. H. and Wilkins, L.** Radioiodine uptake in the study of different types of hypothyroidism in childhood. Pediatrics 12: 288, 1953.

78. **Wilkins, L. and Cara, J.** Further studies on the treatment of congenital adrenal hyperplasia with cortisone. V. Effects of cortisone therapy on testicular development. J. Clin. Endocrinol. & Metab. 14:287, 1954.

79. **Wilkins, L., Clayton, G. M. and Berthrong, M.** The development of goiters in cretins without iodine deficiency. Hypothyroidism due to apparent inability of the thyroid gland to synthesize thyroxine. Pediatrics 13: 235, 1954.

80. **Bongiovanni, A.M>.** Detection of corticoid conjugates in human blood. J. Clin. Endocrinol. & Metab. 14: 341, 1954.

80a. **Bongiovanni, A. M., Eberlein, W. R., Grumbach, M. M. Van Wyk, J. J. and Clayton, G.** Conjugates of adrenal corticoids in human plasms. Proc. Soc. Exper. Biol. & Med. 87: 282, 1954.

81. **Wilkins, L., Bongiovanni, A. M., Clayton, G. W., Grumbach, M. M. and Van Wyk, J. J.** The present status of the treatment of virilising adrenal hyperplasia with cortisone. Experience of 3-1/2 years. Mod. Prob. in Ped., S. Karger, Basel, Switz., 1: 329, 1954.

82. **Bongiovanni, A. M., Eberlein, W. R. and Cara, Jose.** Studies on the metabolism of adrenal steroids in the adrenogenital syndrome. J. Clin. Endocrinol. & Metab. 14: 409, 1954.

83. **Bongiovanni, A. M. and Clayton, G. W., Jr.** A simplified method for the routine determination of pregnamedial and pregnanetriol in urine. Bull. Johns Hopkins Hosp. 94: 180, 1954.

84. **Wilkins, L.** Tools and methods of diagnosis and new trends in the treatment of endocrine disorders. (Borden Award Lecture Pediatrics 13: 393, 1954.

85. **Bongiovanni, A. M. and Clayton, G. W., Jr.** A simplified method for the estimation of 11-oxygenated neutral 17-ketosteroids in the urine of individuals with adrenocortical hyperplasia. Proc. Soc. Exper. Biol. & Med. 85: 428, 1954.

86. **Wilkins, L., Bongiovanni, A. M., Clayton, G. W., Grumbach, M. M. and Van Wyk, J. J.** Virilising adrenal hyperplasia: its treatment with cortisone and the nature of the steroid abnormalitites. Ciba Foundation Colloq. Endocrin. 8: 480, 1954.

87. **Wilkins, L., Grumbach, M. M. and Van Wyk, J. J.** Chromosomal sex in ovarian agenesis. J. Clin. Endocrinol. & Metab. 14: 1270, 1954.

1955

88. **Wilkins, L.** The evolution of endocrine diagnosis and treatment. (Addison Lecture) Gay's Hospital Gasette - March, 1955.

88a. **Wilkins, L.** Endocrine Factors in Obesity in Fat Metabolism, ed. by Najjar, Johns Hopkins Press, Baltimore, 1954.

89. **Wilkins, L.** Hormonal influence on skeletal growth. Ann. N. Y. Acad. Sc. 60: 763, 1955.

90. **Grumbach, M. M., Bongiovanni, A. M., Eberlein, W., Van Wy, J. J. and Wilkins, L.** Cushing's Syndrome with bilateral adrenal hyperplasia: a study of the plasma 17-OH-CS and the response to ACTH. Bull. Johns Hopkins Hosp. 96: 116, 1955.

91. **Wilkins, L., Grumbach, M. M., Van Wyk. J. J., Shepard, T. H., II and Papedatos, C.** Hermaphroditism: classification, diagnosis, selection of sex and treatment. Pediatrics 16: 287, 1955.

92. **Grumbach, M. N., Van Wyk, J. J. and Wilkins, L.** Chromosomal sex in gonadal dyagenesis (ovarian agenesis). Relationship to male pseudohermaphroditism and theories of human sex differentiation. J. Clin. Endocrinol. & Metab. 15: 1161, 1955.

93. **Gyorgy, Wilkins, Hampson et al.** Psychologic aspects of sexual orientation of the child with particular reference to the problem of intersexuality. J. Pediat. 47: 771, 1955.

94. **Van Wyk, J. J.** The use of thyroid in pediatric practice. Quart. Rev. Ped. 10: 212, 1955.

95. **Newberry, E. and Van Wyk, J. J.** A technique for quantitative urine collection in the metabolic study of infants and young children. Pediatriecs 16: 667, 1955.

96. **Hampson, Joan G.** Hermaphreditic genital appearane, rearing and eroticism in hyperadrenocorticism. Bull. Johns Hopkins Hosp. 96: 265, 1955.

97. **Hampson, J. L., Hampson, J. G. and Money, J.** The syndrome of gonadal agensis (ovarian agenesis) and male chromosomal pattern in girls and women. Psychologic studies. Bull. Johns Hopkins Hosp: 97: 207, 1955.

98. **Money, J.** Hermaphroditism, gender and precocity in hyperadrenocorticism. Bull. Johns Hopkins Hosp. 96: 253, 1955.

99. **Money, J., Hampson, J. G. and Hampson, J. L.** An examination of some basis sexual concepts: the evidence of human hermaphroditism. Bull. Johns Hopkins Hosp. 97: 301, 1955.

100. **Money, J.** Hermaphroditism: recommendations concerning assignment of sex, change of sex and psychologic management. Bull. Johns Hopkins Hosp. 97: 284, 1955.

100a. **Money, J. and Hampson, J. G.** Idiopathic sexual precocity in the male. Psychosom. Med. 17: 1, 1955.

100b. **Hampson, J. G. and Money, J.** Idiopathic sexual precocity in the female. Psychosom. Med. 17: 16, 1955.

1956

101. **Childs, B., Grumbach, M. M. and Van Wyk, J. J.** Virilising adrenal hyperplasia: a genetic and hormonal study. J. Clin. Invest. 35: 213, 1956.

102. **Wilkins, L.** The influence of the endocrine glands upon growth and development. Chapter IX in Textbook of Endocrinology, 2nd Ed. R. H. Williams, Saunders, 1955.

103. **Van Wyk, J. J., Grumbach, M. M., Shepard, T. H., II and Wilkins, L.** Treatment of hyperthyroidism with thieuracil drugs. Pediatrics 17: 221, 1956.

104. **Grumbach, M. M. and Wilkins, L.** The pathogenesis and treatment of virilizing adrenal hyperplasia. Pediatrics 17: 418, 1956.

105. **Van Wyk, J. J.** Hypothyroidism in childhood. Pediatrics 17: 427, 1956.

106. **Migeon, C. J., Prystowsky, H., Grumbach, M. M. and Byron, M.** Placental passage of 17-OH-CS: comparison of the levels in maternal and fetal plasma and effect of ACTH and hydrocortisone administration. J. Clin. Invest. 35: 488, 1956.

107. **Hinrichs, E. N., Jr.** Dental changes in idiopathic juvenile hypoparathyroidism. Oral Surg., Oral Med. and Oral Path. 9: 1102, 1956.

108. **Money, J., Hampson, J. O. and Hamson, J. L.** Sexual incongruities and psychopathology. The evidence of human hermaphroditism. Bull. John Hopkins Hosp. 98: 43, 156.

109. **Hampson, J. G., Money, J. and Hampson, J. L.** Hermaphroditism, recommendations concerning case management. J. Clin. Endocrinol. & Metab. 16: 547, 1956.

110. **Money, J.** Psychologic studies oin hypothyroidism, recommendations for case management. Arch. Neurol. & Psych. 76: 296, 1956.

1957

111. **Wilkins, L.** The Diagnosis and Treatment of Endocrine Disorders in Childhood and Adolescence. Springfield, Chas. C. Thomas, 1957.

112. **Mosier, H. D.** Comparative histological study of the adrenal cortex of the wild and domesticated Norway rat. Endocrinology 60: 460, 1957.

113. **Wilkins, L.** Presidential Address. May 31, 1957. Endocrinology 61: 206, 1957.

114. **Smith, D. W, Blizzard, R. M. and Wilkins, L.** The mental prognosis in hypothyroidism of infancy and childhood. A review of 128 cases. Pediatrics 19: 1011, 1957.

115. **Migeon, C. J., Bertrand, J. and Well, P. E.** Physiological disposition of 4-C^{14}-cortisol during late pregnancy. J. Clin. Invest. <u>36</u>: 1350, 1957.

116. **Migeon, C. J., Keller, A. R., Lawrence, B. and Shepard, T. H.** Dehydroepisndrosterone and androsterone levels in human plasma. Effect of age and sex; day-to-day and diurnal variations. J. Clin. Endocrinol. & Metab. <u>17</u>: 1051, 1957.

117. **Migeon, C. J., Bertrand, J., Wall, P. E., Stempfel, R. S. and Prystowsky, H.** Metabolism and placental transmission of cortisol during pregnancy near term. Ciba Colloquia on Endocrinology, 1957.

118. **Migeon, C. J. and Stempfel, R. S.** Laboratory diagnosis in pediatric endorinology. Ped. Clin. of N. A., Nov., 1957, page 959, W.B. Saunders Company.

119. **Blizzard, R. M. and Wilkins, L.** Present concepts of steroid therapy in virilizing adrenal hyperplasia. Arch. Int. Med. <u>100</u>: 729, 1957.

120. **Sandberg, A. A., Eik-Nes, K., Migeon, C. J. and Koepf, G. F.** Plasma 17-hydroxy-corticosteroids in hyperfunction, suppression and deficiency of adrenal cortical function. J. Lab. & Clin. Med. <u>50</u>: 286, 1957.

121. **Bliss, E. L. and Migeon, C. J.** Endocrinology of anorexia nervosa. J. Clin. Endocrinol. & Metab. <u>17</u>: 766, 1957.

1958

122. **Mosier, H. D. and Richter, C.P.** Response of the glomerulosa layer of the adrenal gland of wild and domesticated Norway rats to low and high salt diets. Endocrinology <u>62</u>: 268, 1958.

123. **Mosier, H. D., Blizzard, R. M. and Wilkins, L.** Congenital defects in the biosynthesis of thyroid hormone. Report of two cases. Pediatrics <u>21</u>: 248, 1958.

124. **Stempfel, R. S. and Migeon, C.J.** Precocious and delayed sexual development. Clin. Ob. and Gyn. <u>1</u>: 271, 1958.

125. **Howard, J. E. and Migeon, C. J.** Cushing's Syndrome produced by normal replacement doses of cortisone in a patient with defective mechanism of steroid degradation. Am. J. Med. Sci. <u>235</u>: 387, 1958.

126. **Wilkins, L., Jones, H. W., Jr., Holman, G. H. and Stempfel, R. S., Jr.** Masculinization of the female fetus associated with administration of progestins during gestation: Non-adrenal female pseudohermaphroditism. J. Clin. Endocrinol. & Metab. <u>18</u>: 559, 1958.

127. **Nichols, J., Lescure, O. L. and Migeon, C. J.** The levels of 17-hydroxycorticosteroids and 17-ketosterodis in maternal and cord plasma in term anencephaly. J. Clin. Endocrinol. & Metab. <u>18</u>: 444, 1958.

128. **Martin, M. M. and Wilkins, L.** Pituitary dwarfism: Diagnosis and treatment. J. Clin. Endocrinol. & Metab. <u>18</u>: 679, 1958.

129. **Wilkins, L.** Dysgenesis gonadale et hermaphrodisme. Leurs relations avec les theories de la differenciation sexuelle. Marseille Medical 95: 1, 1958.

130. **Wilkins, L.** Syndrome Adreno-genital. Les Ann. d'Endocrin. <u>19</u>: 841, 1958.

131. **Stempfel, R. S., Jr., Sidbury, J. B., Jr. and Migeon, C. J.** The effects of large doses of salicylate on the metabolism of cortisol in human subjects. (Abstract) Am. J. Dis. Child. <u>96</u>: 543, 1958.

132. **Holman, G. H. and Migeon, C. J.** A functional ensymatic deficiency of cortisol metabolism in young infants. (Abstract) Am. J. Dis. Child. <u>96</u>: 524, 1958.

1959

133. **Migeon, C. J., Wall, P. E. and Bertrand, J.** Some aspects of the metabolism of 16-C^{14}-esterone in normal individuals. J. Clin. Invest. <u>38</u>: 619, 1959.

134. **Wall, P. E. and Migeon, C. J.** In vitro studies with 16-C^{14}-estrone: distribution between plasma and red blood cells of man. J. Clin. Invest. <u>38</u>: 611, 1959.

135. **Gardner, L. I. and Migeon, C. J.** Unusual plasma 17-ketosteroid pattern in a boy with congenital adrenal hyperplasia and periodic fever. J. Clin. Endocrinol. & Metab. <u>19</u>: 266, 1959.

136. **Childs, B., Sidbury, J. B., Jr. and Migeon, C. J.** Glucuronic acid conjugation by patients with familial nonhemolytic jaundice and their relatives. Pediatrics 23: 903, 1959.

137. **Haddad, H. M. and Wilkins, L.** Congenital anomalies associated with gonadal aplasia. Pediatrics 23: 885, 1959.

138. **Blizzard, R. M., Liddle, G. W., Migeon, C. M. and Wilkins, L.** Aldosterone excretion in patients with virilizing adrenal hyperplasia maintained on a normal and low salt diet. J. Clin. Invest. Aug:38(8): 1442-51, 1959.

139. **Howard, E. and Migeon, C. J.** Sex hormone secretion by the adrenal cortex. In The Adrenocortical Hormones: Their Origin- chemistry, physiology and pharmacology. Editor H.W. Deane. 570-637, Springer Verlag,, 1962.

140. **Migeon, C.J.** Androgens in human plasma. In Symposium on Hormones in Human Plasma. Antoniades, H., Editor, Little Brown, 1960.

141. **Migeon, C.J., Lawrence, B., Bertrand, J. and Holman, G. H.** In vivo distribution of some 17-hydroxycorticosteroids between plasma and red blood cells of man. J. Clin. Endocrinol. & Metab. 19: 1411, 1959.

142. **Migeon, C.J., Lescure, O. and Antoniades, H.** Further in vitro studies with 16-C¹⁴-estrone: distribution between plasma protein fractions and red blood cells of man. J. Clin. Invest.

143. **Migeon, C.J.** Cortisol production and metabolism in the neonate. A.M.A.J. Pediatrics 55:280, 1959

144. **Wilkins, L.** Masculinization of the female fetus due to the use of certain synthetic oral progestins during pregnancy. Arch. d'Anat. Microsc. et Morph. Exp. Dec;48(suppl):313-29, 19 59.

145. **Haddad, Heskel M. and Sidbury, J.B., Jr.** Defect of the Iodinating system in congenital goitrous cretinism: report of a case with biochemical studies. J. Clin. Endocrinol. & Metab. 19: 1446, 1959.

145a. **Albert, A., Burns, E., Hampson, J.** Determination of sex and what to do about it. J. Urol. 81: 13, 1959.

1960

146. **Wilkins, L.** Abnormalities of Sex Differentiation: Classification, Diagnosis, Selection of Gender of Rearing and Treatment. Pediatrics 26: 846, November, 1960.

147. **Wilkins, L.** The thyroid gland. Scientific American 202: 119, 1960.

148. **Wilkins, L.** Masculinization of Female Fetus due to Use of Orally given Progestins. J.A.M.A. 172: 1028, 1960 (March 5).

149. **Wilkins, L.** Diagnosis, Selection of Sex of Rearing and Treatment of Various Types of Abnormal Sex Differentiation. In Clinical Endocirnology, I (N.Y., Grune & Stratton). 437-454, 1960.

150. **Wilkins, L.** Hypothyroidism in Children. In Clinical Endocrinology, I (N.Y., Grune & Stratton). 112-122, 1960.

151. **Green, O.C., Migeon, C.J., and Wilkins, L.** Urinary steroids in the hypertensive form of congenital adrenal hyperplasia. J. Clin. Endocrinol. 20: 929, July, 1960.

152. **Wilkins, L.** The Influence of the Endocrine Glands upon Growth and Development, in Textbook of Endocrinology, 3rd edn., R. H. Williams, Saunders, 1960.

153. **Migeon, C.J., Nicolopoulos, D., and Cornblath, M.** Concentrations of 17-hydroxycorticosterodis in the blood of diabetic mothers and in blood from the umbilical cords of their offspring at the time of delivery. Pediatrics 25: 605, 1960.

154. **Stempfel, R.S., Jr., Sidbury, J. B., Jr., and Migeon, C.J.** Β-Glucuronidase hydrolysis of urinary corticosteroid conjugates: Effect of salicylate glucuronidase as a competing enzyme of enzyme inactivation. JCE&M 20: 814, 1960.

155. **Haddad, Heskel M., and Jones, H.W.** Clitoral Enlargement stimulating pseudohermaphroditism. AMA Journal of Diseases of Children 99: 282, 1960.

156. **Cleveland, W., Green, O.C., Migeon, C.** A Case of Proved Adrenocorticotropin Deficiency. Journal of Ped. 57: 376, 1960.

156a. **Migeon, C.J.** Androgens in Human Plasma. Hormones in Human Plasma edited by Antoniades, H. Little Brown and Company, Boston, Mass., 1960.

156b. **Issacs, James P., Blalock A., and Migeon, C. J.** Catecholamine and 17-hydroxycorticosteroid output in dogs with transplanted adrenal glands. Bull. JHH <u>107</u>: 105, August, 1960.

157. **Park, E.A. and Bongiovanni, A.** Biographies of Wilkins. J. Pediatrics, September, 1960.

158. **Jones, H., Wilkins, L.** The Genital Anomaly with Prenatal Exposure to Progestogens. Fertility and Sterility <u>11</u>: 148, March-April, 1960.

159. **Blizzard, R. M.** Inherited Defects of Thyroid Hormone Synthesis and Metabolsim. Metabolism <u>9</u>: 232, March, 1960.

160. **Green, R. Money, J.** Incongruous Gender Role: Nongenital Manifestations in Prepurbertal Boys. The J. of Nervous and Mental Diseases, <u>130</u>: 160, August, 1960.

161. **Money, J.** Components of Eroticism in Man: Cognitional Rehearsals. Recent Advances in Biological Psychiatry. 210, 1960.

1961

162. **Wilkins, L.** Diagnosis and Treatment of Congenital Virlizing Adrenal Hyperplasia. Postgraduate of Medicine <u>29</u>: 31, 1961.

163. **Shulman, L.E., Calkins, E., Cluff, L., and Wilkins, L.** Adrenocortical Steroid Therapy (A Panel Discussion) Md. State Med.J., May, 1961.

164. **Green, O.C., Cleveland, W.W., and Wilkins, L.** Triamcinolone therapy in the adrenaogenital syndrome. Pediatrics <u>27</u>: 292, February, 1961.

165. **David, R. R., Alexander, D.S. and Wilkins, L.** Placental Transfer of an organic radiopaque medium resulting in a prolonged elevation of the protein bound iodine. J. of P. August, 1961, <u>59</u>: 223.

166. **Money, J.** Hermaphroditism. The Encyclopedia of Sexual Behavior. 472, 1961.

167. **Green, R., Money, J.** Effeminacy in Prepubertal Boys. Summary of 11 Cases and Recommendations for Case Management. <u>27</u>: 286, February, 1961.

168. **Money, J.** Components of eroticism in Man. I. The hormones in relation to sexual morphology and sexual desire. J. Nerv. and Mental Dis. <u>132</u>: 239, 1961.

169. **Migeon, C. J., Bertrand, J., Gemzell, C.A.** The Transplacental Passage of Varioous Steroid Hormones in Mid Pregnancy. Present Progress in Hormone Research. 17: 207, 1961.

170. **Migeon, C.J.** The Endocrine Function of the Newborn. CIBA Found. Symposium on Somatic Stability in the Newly Born. 1961. P. 215-237.

1962

171. **Migeon, C. J., Bertrand, J. and Gemzell, C. A.** The Transplacental Passage of Various Steroid Hormones in Med Pregnancy. Recent Progress in Hormone Research. 17: 207, 1961. Also in the Human Adrenal Cortex. Currie Symington and Grant, Editors, Edinburgh, London, 1962.

172. **Cleveland, W. W., Green, O.C., and Wilkins, L.** Deaths in Congenital Adrenal Hyperplasia. Pediatrics. 29: 3, January, 1962.

173. **Aceto, T., Blizzard, R., and Migeon, C.J.** Adrenocortical Insufficiency in Infants and Children. The Ped. Clinics of N. Amer. 9: I, Feb., 1962.

174. **Wilkins, L.** The Effects of Thyroid Deficiency Upon the Development of the Brain. Vol. XXXIX. P. 150-155. Research in Nervous and Mental Disease, 1962.

175. **Cleveland, W.W., Nikesic, M., and Migeon, C.J.** Response to an 11-Hydroxylase Inhibitor (SU-4885) in Patients with Adrenal Hyperplasia and Their Parents. J. Clin. Endocrinol. Metab 22: 281, 1962.

176. **Howard, E. and Migeon, C.J.** Sex Hormone Secretion By the Adrenal Cortex. Handbuch Der Experimentallen Pharmakologie Vol. 14: 560-624. Springer-Verlag, Heidelberg, 1962.

177. **Wilkins, L.** Adrenal Disorders. I. Cushing's Syndrome and Its Puzzles. Arch. Dis. Childhood 37: I, 1962. II. Virilizing Adrenal Hyperplasia. Arch. Dis. Childhood 3: 231, 1962.

178. **Bergada, C., Cleveland, W. W., Jones, H. W., and Wilkins, L.** Gonaldal Histology in Patients with Male Pseudohermaphroditism and Atypical Gonadal Dysgenesis: Relation to Theories of Sex Differentiation. Acta Endocrinologica. 40: 493-520, 1962.

179.Bergada, C., Cleveland, W. W., Jones, H. W., and Wilkins, L. Variants of Embryonic Testicular Dysgenesis: Bilateral Anorchia and the Syndrome of Rudimentary Testes. Acta Endocrinologica. 40: 521-536, 1962.

180. Hung, W., Wilkins, L. and Blizzard, R.M. Medical Therapy of Thyrotoxicosis in Children. Pedatrics 30: 1, July 1962.

181. Chandler, R. W., Kyle, M. A., Hung, W., and Blizzard, R. M. Experimentally Induced Autoimmunization Disease of the Thyroid. I. The Failure of Transplacental Transfer of Anti-Thyroid Antibodies to Produce Cretinism. 40:6, Pediatrics, June 1962.

182. Oh, W., Baens, G. S., Migeon, C. J., Wybregt, S. H., and Cornblath, M. Studies of Carbohydrate Metabolism in the Newborn Infant. V. The Effects of Cortisol on the Hyperglycemic Response to Glucagon. Pediatrics 30: 763, 1962.

183. Rappaport, R., and Migeon, C. J. Physiological Disposition of 4-C^{14}-Tetrahydrocortisol in Man. J. Clin. Endocrinol. Metab. 22: 1065, 1962.

184. Migeon, C. J., Lescure, O. L., Zinkham, W. H., and Sidbury, J. B. In Vitro Interconversion of 16-C^{14}-Estrone and 16-C^{14}-Estradiol-17 β by Erythrocytes from Normal Subjects and From Subjects with a Deficiency of Red Cell Glucose-6-Phospate Dehydrogenase Activity. J. Clin. Invest. 41: 2025, 1962.
Also presented at the First International Congress of Endocrinology, Copenhagen, 1960.

185. Wilkins, L. Modern Materia Medica (Presidential Address). American Pediatric Society. Am. J. Dis. Child 104: 449, 1962.

1963

186. Kenny, F. M., Malvaux, P., and Migeon, C. J. Cortisol Production Rate in Newborns, Infants, and Children. Pediatrics 31: 360, 1963.
Also presented at the 32nd meeting of the Society for Pediatric Research, Atlantic City, May 8-10, 1962. AMA J. Dis. Child 104: 529, 1962.

187. Migeon, C. J., Green, O.C., and Eckert, J. P. Study of Adrenocortical Function in Obesity. Metabolism 12: 718, 1963.

Also presented at the 43rd meeting of the Endocrine Society, New York, June 1961.
188. **Camacho, A. M. and Migeon, C. J.** Isolation, Identification, and Quantification of Testosterone in the Urine of Normal Adults and in Patients with Endocrine Disorders. J. Clin. Endocrinol. l Metab. 23: 301, 1963.
Also presented at the 44th meeting of the Endocrine Society, Chicago, June 1962.
189. **Hung, W., Migeon, C. J., and Parrott, R.M.** A Possible Autoimmune Basis for Addison's Disease in Three Siblings, One with Idiopathic Hypoparathyroidism, Pernicious Anemia, and Superficial Moniliasis. New Eng., J. Med 269: 658, 1963.
190. **Hung, W., Blizzard, R. M., Migeon, C. J., Nyhan, W. and Comacho, A.M.** Precocious Puberty in a Boy with a Hepatoma and Circulating Gonadotropin. J. Pediatrics 63: 895, 1963.

1964

191. **Camacho, A. M. and Migeon, C. J.** Studies of the Origin of Testosterone in the Urine of Normal Adult Subjects and Patients with Various Endocrine Disorders. J. Clin. Invest. 43: 1083, 1964.
192. **Kowarski, A., Finkelstein, J. W., Loras, B., and Migeon, C. J.** The In Vivo Stability of the Tritium Label in 1, 2-H³-Aldosterone Secretion Rate by the Double Isotope Dilution Technique. Steroids 2: 95, 1964.

1965

193. **Finkelstein, J. W., Kowarski, A., Spaulding, J. S., and Migeon, C. J.** Effect of Various Preparations of Human Growth Hormone on Aldosterone Secretion Rate of Hypopituitary Dwarfs. Am. J. Med. 38: 517, 1965.
194. **David, R. R., Bergada, C., and Migeon, C. J.** Isolation, Identification and Measurement of 3α, 17α-Dihydroxypregnane-11, 20-Dione in Congenital Adrenal Hyperplasia. J. Clin. Endocrinol. Metab. 25: 322, 1965.
195. **Bowen, P., Lee, C.S.N., Migeon, C. J., Kaplan, N. M., Whalley, P.J., McKusick, V. A., and Reifenstein, E. C.** Hereditary Male Pseudohermaphroditism with

Hypogonadism, Hypospadias and Gynecomastia (Reifenstein's Syndrome). Annals of Internal Medicine 62: 252, 1965.

196. **Aarskog, D., Blizzard, R. M. and Migeon, C. J.** The Response to Methopyrapone (SU-4885) and Pyrogen Tests in Idiopathic Hypopituitary Dwarfism. J. Clin. Endocrinol. Metab. 25: 439, 1965.

197. **David, R. R., Bergada, C., and Migeon, C. J.** Effect of Age on Urinary Steroid Excretion in Congenital Adrenal Hyperplasia. Bull. Johns Hopkins Hosp. 117: 16, 1965.

198. **Kowarski, A., Finkelstein, J. W., Spaulding, J. S., Holman, G. H., and Migeon, C. J.** Aldosterone Secretion Rate in Congenital Adrenal Hyperplasia. J. Clin. Invest. 44: 1505, 1965.

199. **Migeon, C. J. and Baulieu, E.** Hyperplasie Congenitale Des Surrenales-Etde Biologique. Les Trouble Congenitaux de l'hormogenese. Doin and Masson Ed. Paris, 1965. Presented at VIII Reunion des Endocrinologistes deLangue Francaise, Paris, June 1965.

200. **Kenny, F. M., Preeyasombat, C., and Migeon, C. J.** Cortisol Production Rate. II. Normal Infants, Children, and Adults. Pediatrics 37: 34, 1966.

201. **Rivarola, M. A. and Migeon, C. J.** A Method for the Determination of Cortisol Secretion Rate in Patients Receiving Antibiotics. Bull. Johns Hopkins Hosp. 17: 286, 1965.

202. **Snipes, C. A., Becker, W. G., and Migeon, C. J.** The Effect of Age on the In Vitro Metabolism of Androgens by Guinea Pig Testies. Steroids 6: 771, 1965.

1966

203. **Kowarski, A., Bernant, M., Grossman, M.S. and Migeon, C. J.** Antidiuretic Property of Aldactone (spironolactone) in Diabetes Insipidus. Studies on the Mechanism of Antidiuresis. Bull. Johns Hopkins Hosp. 119: 413, 1966.

204. **Kenny, F. M., Preeyasombat, C., Spaulding, J. S. and Migeon, C. J.** Cortisol Production Rate. IV. Infants Born of Steroid-Treated Mothers and of Diabetic Mothers. Infants with Trisomy Syndrome and with Anencephaly. Pediatrics 37: 960, 1966.

205. **Becker, W. G., Snipes, C. A. and Migeon, C. J.** Progesterone-4-C^{14}. Metabolism to Androgens by Testes of Normal and Isoimmune Aspermatogenic Guinea Pigs. Endocrinology 78: 737, 1966.

206. **Rivarola, M. A. and Migeon, C. J.** Determination of Testosterone and Androst-4-Ene-3, 17-Dione Concentration in the Human Plasma. Steroid 7: 103, 1966.